EASY BREEZY
PROSPERITY

EASY BREEZY PROSPERITY

THE FIVE FOUNDATIONS FOR A MORE JOYFUL, ABUNDANT LIFE

EMMANUEL DAGHER

RODALE.

RODALE
wellness
Live happy. Be healthy. Get inspired.

Sign up today to get exclusive access to our authors, exclusive bonuses, and the most authoritative, useful, and cutting-edge information on health, wellness, fitness, and living your life to the fullest.

Visit us online at RodaleWellness.com
Join us at RodaleWellness.com/Join

This book is intended as a reference volume only, not as a medical manual. The information given here is designed to help you make informed decisions about your health. It is not intended as a substitute for any treatment that may have been prescribed by your doctor. If you suspect that you have a medical problem, we urge you to seek competent medical help.

The information in this book is meant to supplement, not replace, proper exercise training. All forms of exercise pose some inherent risks. The editors and publisher advise readers to take full responsibility for their safety and know their limits. Before practicing the exercises in this book, be sure that your equipment is well-maintained, and do not take risks beyond your level of experience, aptitude, training, and fitness. The exercise and dietary programs in this book are not intended as a substitute for any exercise routine or dietary regimen that may have been prescribed by your doctor. As with all exercise and dietary programs, you should get your doctor's approval before beginning.

Mention of specific companies, organizations, or authorities in this book does not imply endorsement by the author or publisher, nor does mention of specific companies, organizations, or authorities imply that they endorse this book, its author, or the publisher.

Internet addresses and telephone numbers given in this book were accurate at the time it went to press.

Rodale books may be purchased for business or promotional use or for special sales. For information, please write to:
Special Markets Department, Rodale Inc., 733 Third Avenue, New York, NY 10017

Printed in the United States of America
Rodale Inc. makes every effort to use acid-free ♾, recycled paper ♻.

Book design by Christina Gaugler

Library of Congress Cataloging-in-Publication Data is on file with the publisher.

ISBN 978-1-62336-621-6 hardcover

Distributed to the trade by Macmillan

2 4 6 8 10 9 7 5 3 1 hardcover

RODALE.

We inspire and enable people to improve their lives and the world around them.

For my amazing mom Emili, and my family—
Cyril, Ziad, and Michael.

Thank you for your unconditional love, support, and presence in my life.

And for you, my reader and friend.

Thank you for allowing me to be a part of your journey into greater prosperity. May your abundance be multiplied manyfold and fully enjoyed. This or something greater, and so it is!

CONTENTS

Foreword

FOR MORE THAN three and a half decades, I have been studying success. I have read thousands of books on the subject, traveled the world attending seminars by the greatest masters in the industry, listened to more audio programs that you can imagine, and now I am blessed to run a business in the same industry, sharing profound and centuries-old truths. I've even written a few books on the subject, and here's what I love about Emmanuel's book *Easy Breezy Prosperity* . . . he pleasantly surprised me with a new way of viewing prosperity. He opened up my imagination and consciousness to techniques I've never heard of or read about ANYWHERE! Emmanuel makes prosperity so easy . . . easy to understand, easy to implement, and easy to enjoy.

We truly do live in an abundant universe. If we took all of the money in the world and divided it evenly among all of the people, there would be plenty for everyone. If we took all of the food in the world and divided it evenly, there would be plenty of food for everyone. It is your birthright to be prosperous and to enjoy prosperity.

Perhaps you were raised in an environment that was filled with prosperity and your role models had a healthy relationship with money. Or maybe you were raised in an environment like mine, which was impoverished. My parents both worked multiple jobs to put food on the table for our family of six. If we wanted something, we were told things like, "What, do you think I'm *made* of money?!"

Growing up with a lack mentality is the way most people are raised, but fortunately, it isn't the way you have to live your life. Whether you are new to these philosophies or you've been studying them for quite some time, you will still discover a unique approach to prosperity in this book.

One of the reasons why most people don't see a change in their environment is because they don't receive the proper guidance. *Easy Breezy Prosperity* gives you that guidance and the processes that you can implement immediately.

You will discover a great deal about your relationship with money and determine whether your relationship is one that is nurturing or destructive. This one concept alone could drastically change your results. But there is so much more for you to uncover within these pages.

Emmanuel will have you looking at prosperity in a new light . . . a much brighter one that will illuminate your life in beautiful ways. He claims, "Many cultures focus so heavily on superficial forms of success that they overlook the real meaning behind the idea."

As you study this book, be open to the new awareness. Dedicate yourself to investing quality time with this book. Rather than simply reading the book, putting it aside, and saying "great book," allow this book to be a daily study. Contemplate the ideas, follow through on the processes, and have fun with it.

Life is meant to be fun. And, frankly, when you are in the state of joy (which you'll be in when you are having fun), you are attracting and inviting even more prosperity into your life.

You will find that the more you share these ideas with others, the more good will be returned to you. There is a natural law of the universe that decrees that the more good you put out, the more you'll get back.

Study, implement, and share! My wish for you is an abundant and joy-filled life.

Peggy McColl
New York Times best-selling author
peggymccoll.com

Introduction

GREETINGS, my prosperous friend!

This book is the realization of more than a dozen years of experience in helping people create greater prosperity and well-being in their lives. I am deeply honored to have the opportunity to share with you all of the knowledge I have acquired when it comes to creating a more prosperous life.

Within this book you will be presented with a variety of simple yet paradigm-shifting concepts and practical ways to expand your own prosperity and success.

Are you ready?

Throughout my many joyous years as a prosperity coach and wellness practitioner, I have connected with and befriended thousands of people from all over the world who are seeking their own personal transformation. I have met many people who are eager and excited to change but with no idea of where or how to start, while others run themselves through a sometimes overwhelming amount of self-empowerment reading and spiritual guidance before the Universe brings our paths together. Nearly all of my clients have in common their search for their higher self and a desire for greater happiness and prosperity.

This powerful guide to prosperity will help you to realize the success you've already created in your life, cultivate the clarity needed to create your greatest life path, and define what prosperity is—and how to attract more of it.

Together, we will journey through an extraordinary transformation and focus on creating a positive approach to generating greater wealth.

Many cultures focus so heavily on superficial forms of success that they overlook the real meaning behind the idea. Prosperity is too often seen as a purely monetary matter. In this book, we are going to move well beyond that misconception. Simply by reading this book, you've already placed yourself at a crossroads. Behind you is your old life, while in all directions, in front of and beside you, lie future prosperity and expansion.

There is no turning back now, only forward momentum.

The laws of physics state that energy can't be created or destroyed, only changed. Life is energy; we are all energy—our thoughts, feelings, actions—everything around us comes from the cosmos. We are all connected to one another by the limitless energy of the Universe. When we acknowledge this, we open ourselves up to infinite possibilities for extraordinary growth.

Science and spirituality have been at odds with each other for a long time, and we are only now approaching a time when they are beginning to meld and mold into each other. What a fantastic time to be alive! As both spiritual and scientific beings, we have often felt as if we had to choose a side; that time is now at an end.

We can be conscious of the energies around us and how they interact, while still maintaining an open and inviting atmosphere in our hearts, minds, and personal space. When we open ourselves up to the energies of love, change, gratitude, and prosperity, the Universe rewards us by magnifying the possibilities that bring more of these energies into our lives. Through receiving these energies, we also allow ourselves to project them back out into the Universe and toward all of the people, places, and experiences around us.

Spreading these wonderful energies not only brings happiness, joy, and love to our friends and family, it also creates a feedback loop of positivity and attraction. The higher the frequency of energy that we share, the more of that energy we attract back to ourselves.

This book would not exist if it weren't for YOU, my extraordinary reader. The success of my first book, *Easy Breezy Miracle,* and the energy that all my amazing readers bring to my work, has enabled this book to manifest. I cannot thank you enough for all of the support and loving energies you have brought into my life. It is in exchange, in thanks, and in the name of expansion, that I share with you *Easy Breezy Prosperity.*

It was in response to your collective call for a life-changing yet simple guide that led me to create this book about my own and others' experiences with prosperity, and to share the tools that have helped thousands create more wealth in their daily lives. I have written this book so that you too can have access to these powerful processes, which will help you in creating your own prosperity. I can only hope that you will share your knowledge after reading this book, to help others to pursue their dreams and make them a reality.

I am certain that by consistently using some of the insights and prosperity processes provided in this book, you will begin to attract more success and prosperity into your life. Make the information in this book a part of your personal practice, and have fun with it.

The knowledge that I share here are the processes, ideas, and tools that I have incorporated and apply daily in my own life. There is nothing here that I don't stand by personally.

I want nothing more than for you to create a prosperous reality for yourself out of your deepest desires for change.

Are you ready for a life full of easy breezy prosperity?

Why I'm So Passionate About Helping You Prosper

People often ask me questions like, "What makes you so passionate about inspiring and empowering people to prosper?" Or "You're so positive and seem to enjoy life to the fullest. How did you get to be that way, and why is it so easy for you?"

To answer these questions, I think it's important to take you on a little journey through some of the experiences of my early life. My story does not define who I am. But the experiences I've had, starting when I was very young, have helped to shape my deep drive to help humanity align with their greatest potential. I look at every experience I've ever faced, even the challenging ones, as blessings that have allowed me to develop a deep compassion and love for humanity. Empowering others is not a job for me; it's a way of life.

So it is with great joy and humility that I share in a bit more detail how and why I chose this path of service. I hope it gives you a clearer understanding of why offering my love, dedication, and support to contribute to your happiness and prosperity is such a priority for me.

It has often been stated that the first decade of a person's life is the most critical, because that is when the brain is passing through its most delicate developmental stages. This period of time usually lays the groundwork for our ability to maintain a core inner strength and shapes our identity, as we navigate through childhood and into adolescence. During this time, the foundations are laid that will shape much of who we will become as adults.

Looking back at the first 10 years of my own childhood, I realize that the experiences I had then were helping me to develop an ongoing state of inner strength and resilience. Hidden in those years was the gift of my being able to experience the incredible freedom and abundance I have in my life today. Of course, as many people experience in life, those lessons could be very challenging. Let me explain what I mean by sharing a bit of my background.

The first memory I can recall in this lifetime is of sitting with my mother on the cold cement floor of a convent, when I was three years old. We would both sit and sleep on that floor, in a bedroom that belonged to one of the nuns at the convent in Jouret el Termos, a city just outside the capital city of Beirut, Lebanon. That convent was our home for seven years during the Lebanese Civil War.

We fled to the convent when our mother realized that our own home was no longer safe for us to live in. I am still amazed at how blessed we were to have even gotten safely inside those convent doors, because the nuns never opened their doors to anyone from outside the church. But because they knew that my mom was a wonderful schoolteacher, they made an exception in our case and let us come in. They hired her to assist the other teachers in the school as needed. Of course there wasn't much school going on during those days of war, so we felt there must have been a higher power watching over us. What was also quite extraordinary is that I was the only boy who was allowed to live there. The convent was built like a fortress, so it was one of the safest places for us to be in that city.

On the other side of the wall, outside the convent, were the terrible sights and sounds of the Lebanese Civil War, which raged from 1975 to 1990. The conflict was particularly active during the 1980s, when I was a young child.

Our bed was a thin blanket that we shared, spread over the concrete floor. The convent had no running hot water and very little electricity, and the nuns were only able to feed us pita bread and water each day. But we found our own inspiration and held one another together with promises that we would make it out safely.

To keep our spirits up and pass the time, my mother and I would sing songs that we loved. We sang in soft whispering voices, so we wouldn't give away our presence to anyone on the street outside. We had one VHS tape, the classic film *The Sound of Music.* I think I must have seen that movie a thousand times. It's kind of funny, because the story begins at a convent, where Maria is planning on becoming a full-fledged nun, and the story unfolds just as WWII is breaking out. So her story of living in a convent—and hiding there at one point as she and her family become refugees from war—was similar to our own circumstances.

I think that is when my love for music really began. I could identify with the character of Maria as being a free spirit. I felt that same impulse for freedom and creative expression myself, so her story was very comforting to me and to my mother. That movie helped us get through a lot of rough days.

The convent room we lived in had a barred window, similar to the ones they had in prisons and castles centuries ago. I could see the scenes of war happening right outside that little window, which meant that I had to grow up very quickly. There was a thickness you could feel in the air that had a relentless, nauseating effect. It permeated the city and did not let up for many years.

I remember how it felt to be three years old and living amid the sounds of bombs, tanks, and firefights on the other side of the convent wall. We lived in the moment; life was very uncertain. But I made a deal with myself then, at age three. I promised myself and God that if my mom and I were able to make it out of the war safely, I would spend the rest of my life trying to help others, to make the world a more positive and wonderful place to live.

I got through it all by singing, creating magical "escape stories" with my mom, and saying many prayers. Within the convent, no one talked about the war, because we were all living it. It was not something people discussed, because it was so hard to deal with the fact that it was happening all around us, unrelentingly. If we'd talked about it, it would have become overwhelming. It sounds strange to people who have not been through this, but there is an unspoken acknowledgment among those experiencing a war, that they will work hard to live as positively and normally as possible and not steep themselves in the awful reality happening on the streets outside. In England during World War II, children who were evacuated from their schools or homes often carried on with their schoolwork as well as they could, wherever they were—in air raid shelters, pubs, garages, church halls, or emergency schools. Life has to go on.

Of course everyone was still experiencing the war, even though we didn't discuss it. The interesting thing is, that although I could feel my mother's fear and the fear of everyone around me at the time, I always had a sense of inner peace and trust that everything was going to be okay. I believe now that these two components of inner peace and trust are what helped me build my own inner core of strength. They are also a huge part of anyone's abundance. These experiences taught me, at an age when I was still trying to understand language and everyday life, that the only real and lasting peace is that which we experience within and create from within. Being a child, I found that peace inside myself far more easily than the adults around me, who had been taught to think in terms of outer circumstances, even if they viewed life in a spiritual way. I was freer to realize the deeper truth—that our lives always come from within, and how we meet and create our outer lives only ever comes down to how we experience our own inner life.

In that sense, I was at an advantage, being a child. In fact, my mom often tells me that it was as if I was *her* parent most of the time. I would have her rest her head on my shoulder and would affirm that everything was going to be OK. I would assure her that a greater presence was watching over us and keeping us safe.

She often tells me that those words, along with my ability to make her laugh during the little song-and-dance performances I would put on for her, are what got her through those challenging, uncertain times.

Finally, after my mother and I had been in the convent for seven years, living only on pita bread and water and sleeping on a cement floor, we were able to escape the combat zone. We took advantage of a brief break in the civil war to leave the convent and the city behind for good. To me, leaving the convent was great but also scary, because it had been our refuge and safe haven for so long. But it was meant to be.

We experienced one miraculous form of help after

another—our escape is a miraculous story in and of itself, which I will tell more fully in another book. And because of those miracles, we were able to escape the war and leave Lebanon completely. We never looked back.

My family and I were able to escape to the nearby island of Cyprus. During our brief stay there, we were able to get visas to come to the United States, where some of our family members lived. We moved straight to the Midwest, to a quiet farming town in Indiana, where my aunt had married a local man. We were able to live with my aunt and her husband until my mom and stepdad (my mom had remarried at this point) were able to get on their feet financially.

I was almost 11 years old by the time we moved to the United States, and because the Lebanese Civil War had already started when I was born, the move to America was the first time I had ever experienced peace and silence in my outer world. My new home was a complete 180 degree turn from the life we had known in Lebanon. Our new town was in a rural area with an open sky and flat land, with fields of corn that stretched out for miles. It was as though the Universe knew exactly what kind of peaceful, natural environment I needed then, so that I could move through and heal the trauma I had experienced in Lebanon.

This period of time would also come to influence how I viewed money and prosperity. These were issues that I later needed to work through, because like many children, I saw my parents struggle in a big way to make enough money to make ends meet. We had completely started over in a new land and had to learn a new language and a whole new culture. Everything was new and different in those first few years in a new country. But we made it, and like the rest of my family, I'm so grateful! It completely changed our lives to be able to come to the United States and start over in a peaceful place. That was a tremendous part of our abundance, to realize how blessed we were in our new home.

The transition was interesting for me, especially at school, because at the time I was one of only two people in the entire school system who was a minority member. I had to go the extra mile to try to "fit in" and be accepted socially. But it was definitely a good experience and one that grounded me. Those years gave me the space and time to heal from the daily trauma of war.

My outlook on life has been powerfully shaped by everything that my family and I went through in living through and escaping the war. That time in my life taught me to fully appreciate and be aware of the present moment, and to appreciate all that I have, knowing how blessed we are for any good thing that we or others are experiencing.

I know that many people are not taught to be appreciative of all that they have. They may not see that appreciation in the grownups around them as they are growing up, for the most part. They see worry and stress, as their parents or grandparents express fear or frustration that the bills are piling up, or that one disaster—an illness or lost job—could set them back for years at a time.

Unfortunately, many people living in the wealthier, peaceful parts of the world often don't know how blessed they are. Because so much is available to them and constantly advertised in front of them, they also tend have a very high standard for their outer life. That is understandable—many in the United States and Europe, for example, enjoy a high standard of living, and certainly everyone deserves to live well and abundantly. Abundance is our natural birthright.

But sometimes that high expectation crowds out our appreciation for what we've already achieved or been given. We also have a perfectionist standard, particularly in the United States, so that we're always looking to improve every system, product, and service, to create the best we can possibly create.

That high standard is known around the world, and it is wonderful. That high expectation and people's visions of what they could create have created great nations. But it is not the case for most countries in the world. The opportunities available in a wealthy country are unusually abundant and empowering compared to what most of the world's people experience. It's easy, in a wealthy place, to want to keep moving forward and keep asking for more, to forget to appreciate how far we've already come.

Many Americans and Europeans notice this when they travel to poorer countries. They meet people there who seem to appreciate what they have far more than those in wealthier cultures do. It comes as a surprise to these travelers. They often end up envying the other culture's freedom from constantly wanting things. They also envy how much the people in these countries live in and enjoy the present moment.

Sometimes we can also get caught up in our dreams for the future—our visions of what can be. When that happens, it's easy for our minds to mainly notice what's *not* working in our lives, instead of what is. This can lead us to complain to ourselves and those around us about everything that's wrong, which only affirms what we *don't* want. It also leaves us with the feeling that our lives are not on track—that life is hard, that the Universe is not "conspiring on our behalf" the way we would like it to.

When we carry that belief, then when things are going well, it's easy to feel uneasy with that calm feeling and to expect the next disaster to come round the corner at any minute. Many people live in that guarded state, where they swear by "Murphy's Law" that something is about to go wrong. Many grew up in homes where the adults were constantly on the defensive, anticipating the next bad thing that might happen, as if that protected them in some way.

Those beliefs are natural and understandable for those raised in painful or traumatic circumstances. But they are the opposite of living in joy and gratitude. They also keep us from appreciating the present moment. And when we live that way, we separate ourselves from our natural state of abundance. That defensive stance keeps us from relaxing and appreciating all the gifts we receive every day. It keeps us from opening up to greater levels of prosperity, because we keep affirming that it's "hard enough just to survive." And it warns us away from giving to others, because we feel we barely have enough for ourselves.

I completely understand how anyone could end up in that bind, and my heart goes out to them, with real compassion. But there is another way, and it not hard to learn. It just takes practice.

The whole experience of living in war taught me to appreciate everything I have and everything and everyone around me, and to always look for the blessings in every experience. Just like the inner peace and trust that I experienced as a small child, this has to come from within. Appreciation doesn't come from the place in our ego that is satisfied because we just got what we wanted. It comes from the realization that everything in the Universe flows from a place of love. Even with all the challenges that we experience on this Earth, we are constantly moving forward, always coming to understand more fully why we are here, and remembering our true purpose and mission in life.

That experience also taught me how to be very disciplined in my personal and spiritual practice, and to walk the talk, always! There is no substitute for daily prayer and/or meditation. It is impossible to maintain a higher stance in life, to stay calm and keep everything in perspective, if we don't take a few minutes to ground and center ourselves, and to check in with our guides and angels each morning. We can feel their presence with us throughout the day much more easily if we start off acknowledging their presence and speaking with them or the Universe in general, asking questions and receiving whatever wisdom and encouragement we need each day.

All of us are always moving forward. I see myself as the eternal student. I am always looking to get even more in touch with my most authentic self/spirit. It's a daily journey to find out who we really are and why we are here.

As hard as it was to go through the experience of living with war, I would not change any of it in any way, because I know it made me the person I am today. It gave me the tremendous gift of being present and in the moment, appreciating where I am and all that I have. It gave me the gift of realizing how amazingly abundant I am—I've certainly lived on more than bread and water for many years now!—in addition to living in a lovely home, being healthy, doing work that I love, and having fulfilling relationships.

It gave me the gift of realizing how important it is to hold a steady vision of the blessings I want to receive and to give thanks for these before they arrive, knowing they are already there on the energetic plane and that expecting them to arrive creates them all the more quickly.

It gave me the gift of realizing how blessed I am because of the abundance that is everywhere around us on this beautiful Earth—the beauty of the Earth, the blessings of food and clean water, a safe place to sleep at night, the love of friends and family. It's shown me how much there is to share, and that instead of denying ourselves, when we share, we open up a way to receive more.

I often think back to that time, remembering the promise I made as a small child, that if my mom and I were able to safely escape that war, that for the rest of my life I would do all I could to make the world a more positive place. I kept my word; I have intentionally created a life of service that seeks to encourage and inspire others, through my humanitarian efforts and through my work as an author, teacher, musician, and counselor.

Whenever a challenge comes up in my daily life, I think back to the first 10 years of my life and remember how far I've come. Not only does this put all the events of my life into perspective, both past and present, it also reminds me how blessed I am to have attained safety and freedom from a conflict that so many couldn't escape from on their own, let alone with a beloved family member. It helps me to trust that every challenge in our lives isn't there to knock us down or make us feel discouraged. It's there to make us feel more empowered, to help us expand our inner strength, by helping us see that we create our own world by our intentions and beliefs, as well as our outer actions. Challenging situations are actually a chance to stretch forward in our expectations, to manifest inner peace and trust in the universe on a much higher level. We then begin to develop even greater inner strength and to align even more with our greatest potential.

I share some of my early journey with you not to say, "Look at how great I am!" but to say that we are all, at one time or another, in a very vulnerable place in life. I know what it is to be at the bottom of the bottom, the depths of despair. I slept on a concrete floor for seven years, with only a thin blanket to keep my mother and me warm, living only on pita bread and water, music that inspired us, and the belief that we could at any moment be free to leave and move somewhere safe. Yet I was able to grow up to be happy and healthy, and ended up not only prospering myself but actually helping others to prosper, to take positive steps toward their dreams that would help them manifest their higher vision for their lives.

Believe me: If I can do it, so can you.

I now use my work and my daily life to help others understand that it *can* be done! We can create beautiful, fulfilling, abundant lives, if we follow the Universe's laws (prosperity principles) and allow ourselves to give to ourselves and others, to express gratitude for all we receive, to have support networks that keep us on track, to have clear intentions and a vision of what we want to create, based on our true desires and intuition. Much of what is required is covered in this book, to help you in creating your own beautiful, miraculous life.

Looking at my life from the outside, I was once what some would call a refugee or "victim" of war—and yet, I wasn't. I chose as a child to never fully take on that role, even though I could have easily stepped into it. I am very thankful for that, and yet I saw much in those days that made me grow up very quickly. Because I had to grow up so fast, I learned to think and process experiences like an adult very early on. I lost years of the easygoing, joyful, playful life that all children need and want.

And yet, as an adult, I have increasingly added more play and fun in my life, in part because I see how important it is to live from the heart more than the head. A huge part of claiming our abundance is realizing the miracle of the present moment, in ways that children do so naturally. In some ways, I've grown up in reverse, adding the playful openness of childhood to my everyday experience as an adult. This has actually helped me not to be so "in my head" about life. It has allowed me to stay in the flow, which has greatly contributed to my prosperity.

Eckhart Tolle is a wonderful example of this. He became a millionaire after his books *The Power of Now* and *A New Earth* sold millions of copies around the world. But he didn't prosper because he was actually *trying* to make a lot of money. He's never taken his eye off the miracle and joy of the present moment. And obviously, millions of people agree with him. Life is in feeling and appreciating the Now moment, not our To-Do List!

I was given a great gift at an early age—a beautiful vision of helping others, a sense of purpose and joy, and the energy and imagination to see it through. In complete gratitude for this, I now travel the world, helping people thrive in all areas of their lives. I'm living my dream and choosing to make my audience part of that dream.

I cannot tell you how much that audience (including

you) mean to me. I will continue to cheer all of you on, throughout your journey. Whatever that journey might be, I know it's a beautiful vision. And now you have the tools to create it.

My Previous Experience with Money (And Why I Wrote This Book)

My readers, friends, and family have expressed their absolute need for this book, but I also wanted to write it for another important reason: I wanted to write the book that I myself needed to read 10 years ago. When I was just starting out in my career, I thought that struggling financially was inevitable. I didn't know then that my struggle was a symptom of being out of alignment with my true path.

From a young age, I saw my parents struggle in life. It wasn't because they were bad people, incompetent, or pursuing the wrong ideals—it was because they didn't know how *not* to struggle.

My family and I immigrated to the United States from Lebanon when I was 11. We came here with very little and had to build our lives from nothing. My parents worked hard, day and night, to make sure that there was enough food for my brother and me. My mother, the epitome of generosity, often went without food, new clothes, and new shoes, just so my brother and I would have enough to eat. Like many mothers, she felt she would rather be hungry herself, so that her children could eat and grow up to be strong and healthy. She is the greatest mother anyone could ever ask for.

As I watched my parents struggle to make enough money to survive and still fulfill their dreams, I was conditioned to think that struggle was necessary. I grew to believe that everyday life, and especially our dreams, weren't worth pursuing if they came easily and without a fight. It took years of research and life experience for me to realize that struggling is often a symptom of pursuing the right dream down the wrong path. This doesn't mean that struggles can't be or aren't part of building character and experiencing personal growth. However, an extended struggle is often a sign from the Universe that another path or option may be open to you that you haven't noticed yet.

When I was first pursuing a career, I bought into the idea of the "starving artist," that a person must "pay their dues" in order to succeed, putting forth a great deal of effort and experiencing hard times in order to qualify for success. I didn't see the other opportunities presenting themselves to me because I was too wrapped up in my own struggle and preconceived ideas about what success looked like, and how I was supposed to chase after it.

One of my most powerful "aha!" moments came when I let myself relax and contemplate where I wanted my career to take me—where I wanted the Universe to guide me. It was this experience, combined with the desperation that comes from a true struggle to survive, that allowed me to purposely cultivate my own demeanor of positive energy for the first time in my life.

Before this, I would create a demeanor of positive energy unintentionally or by necessity, but never through purposeful thought and intention. I then realized I needed to generate positive energy in order to attract more positive situations in my life.

Though the struggle I was facing motivated me to change things, it wasn't enough to help me generate the appropriate energy needed to create true prosperity. It was only through refocusing my energy into thoughts and feelings that naturally attract abundance that I was able to let go of my need to struggle. I was then able to pursue my dreams and desires without carrying too much baggage. As difficult as this was, only then was I able to transcend the old energy blocks and create the kind of prosperity I had never thought possible for me.

Part of this transcending and refocusing on more positive energies and a more prosperous outlook involved a change in my perception of money. I hadn't recognized money as spiritual energy. I later learned that money is highly spiritual, in that it's all about giving and receiving—the sharing of energy from one place to another. This doesn't mean that money is religious in nature, but rather that it is a part of our spiritual existence, and a positive force in the world.

Before I began my journey to better understanding money, I didn't see how money fit into the equation regarding the problems I wanted to help solve. I hoped to better the world, to better the planet, and I saw money as only making things worse. This could not be further from the truth. Later on, I'll share with you how I was able to overcome my prejudice against money, and how that shift in thinking greatly improved my finances and my life in general.

This book will teach you how to do the same. It is the book that I so desperately needed years ago, and I can only hope that it will help so many others who are in the same place that I was. I had read every self-help and self-empowerment guide on the market, but none of them were able to completely

open me up to the kind of shifts I was searching for, especially when it came to living a prosperous life. I looked high
and low for this book, but it exists now thanks in part to you,
dear reader.

It was only through my own life experiences, challenges,
and allowing myself to get clear on my true desires, that I was
able to develop the tools necessary to prosper. Once I developed those tools, I put myself in a place where I was capable of
helping others discover these powerful tools and processes for
themselves.

Looking back, I've realized that by opening myself up to
the Universe, I was able not only to pursue prosperity for
myself, but also to assist others seeking their prosperity, which
is one of my greatest personal desires.

Are you ready to pursue a reality flooded with prosperity
and to take this journey with me?

How Easy Breezy Prosperity Works

I've developed five core foundations that can help people open
their lives and energies to prosperity:

Finding Happiness

Embracing Circulation

Investing in Yourself and Creating Balance

Building a Support Network

Practicing Gratitude and Kindness

These principles of prosperity should be considered as
energy foundations that are here for you to build on and
expand. These five foundations are meant to support you in

your personal transformation journey. They are the focal points for all of the methods you will be learning to integrate into your daily routine.

These foundations are the building blocks for inviting positive prosperity frequencies into your life, consciousness, and environment. They are here to support and flow through you, enabling you to fully receive the abundance the world has in store for you. These prosperity principles are simple guidelines, not a rigid set of rules.

After introducing each foundation, I'll arm you with prosperity processes to help you incorporate the tenets of that foundation into your life. These processes are easy, breezy, step-by-step instructions on how to transform prosperity ideas into action. You may find that some processes work better for you than others, which is completely fine. I would encourage you, though, to complete the processes you are less drawn to, as often the processes we are most hesitant to try are the ones we need to do the most; that's definitely how it was for me. Once I embraced those processes, I found myself more bountiful and prosperous than ever before.

Prosperity processes, much like our miracle processes from *Easy Breezy Miracle,* are based in both spirituality and science. They are actions to reinforce the ideas in this book and to help you make the changes necessary to create future successes. Think of these processes as tools in a magical toolbox, waiting to be used for building your prosperity. Each tool is fun and simple to use—I don't believe in overcomplicating things.

Each process and idea should all be considered within the context of 21- and 28-day cycles. As psychologist Jeremy Dean says in his book *Making Habits, Breaking Habits,* it takes 21 days to break a habit and 28 days to establish a new one.[1] Because of this fact, I've included a 28-day plan at the end of the book that you can use as a guide for incorporating the *Easy Breezy Prosperity* foundations and processes into your daily life, until the methods become second nature.

Try not to get too frustrated as you are forming new habits. Our brains need a little extra time and consideration when making big changes. Change can be challenging. It's important to give ourselves plenty of time to adjust to them.

Let's get started!

1 Jeremy Dean, *Making Habits, Breaking Habits* (Boston: De Cappo Lifelong Books, 2013), 3–4.

Finding Your Happiness

Typically, when people think of prosperity, they think of monetary prosperity. They think of how much they have in their bank accounts or how much their car or home is worth. But monetary prosperity is only one kind of prosperity, and even though it's definitely the one people seem most concerned with, it's rarely the most important.

Prosperity is about so much more than the contents of our bank accounts or investment portfolios. Prosperity is about what we achieve and how we look at reality. It's about choosing to operate from a space of knowing that we are enough. We aren't lacking.

If we can acknowledge and accept who we are and where we come from, and operate from there, we are better equipped to overcome any challenges we may face.

In our consumer-driven economy, we tend to measure our self-worth in terms of net worth. Of course, having money makes life easier, but it does not *make* life. It's things like our friends, family, and health that make life worth living.

I once had a client, David, who had been brought up in a wealthy family so he never had to worry about money. Succeeding at school and at work was always what was most important. He was raised to think that if you didn't have a 4.0 GPA or if you weren't running your own company, there was something wrong with you. He came to me feeling unfulfilled in his life and pressured at his job. He wanted advice and help pursuing more prosperity, because he felt he hadn't done enough to make his family proud—despite running a company and having graduated top of his class in business school. He felt his business wasn't performing as well as it could, and he really wanted to make sure he was doing everything possible to ensure it succeeded. David couldn't see how much he did have because he was so focused on what he thought he didn't have.

We worked together for several sessions, identifying what he wanted, what he had, and where he wanted to be in six months. By focusing on what prosperity really is and not assigning a dollar amount, a grade, or a profit margin to it, David and I were able to work out a way for him to feel fulfilled at work, while still being grateful and acknowledging how much he had in his personal life with his family and friends.

By letting go of the purely monetary aspect of prosperity, David was better able to see exactly how prosperous he was! His family was healthy; his work was stimulating. His fears about not being good enough or not being successful enough faded as he learned to enjoy the other aspects of prosperity: pursuing happiness and being grateful for the things you have. With help from exercises in this foundation and others, David learned to evaluate his prosperity and success by how happy he was, not by how much money he made during the quarter, or how many new clients his business took on.

David began to appreciate the smaller things and started to take more time away from work to enjoy time with his family. He allocated time to pursue new hobbies he enjoyed, thereby enabling a healthier work-life balance as he spent less time in the office. David contacted me recently to share with me that he's never been happier, and his business has never been more successful.

The dictionary defines prosperity as "a successful, flourishing, or thriving condition, especially in financial respects; good fortune."[1] Although this is accurate, it's not complete. At its root, prosperity is about happiness. In my experiences with clients and in my own life, I've come to create another definition of prosperity as being "the successful pursuit of happiness; a thriving and flourishing state of being."

Prosperity is overcoming your fear and doubt, making the choice to actively step into your ideal self.

Purpose and Prosperity

One of the most important steps toward prosperity is acknowledging and discovering our purpose. Our purpose in life is more than pursuing that 9-to-5 job, paying off the mortgage, or counting how many friends we have. Our purpose in life, the *meaning* of life, is to be happy.

That's it. All we need to pursue in life is happiness. Through happiness, we will discover prosperity encompassing all the

---

1 "Prosperity," *Dictionary.com Unabridged* (online; Random House, Inc., 2014) http://dictionary.reference.com/browse/prosperity (accessed May 10, 2014).

aspects it entails—family, friends, financial, health, and career. We know our purpose by knowing what brings us joy.

As we search for our true purpose, every choice before us should be simplified down to one question: "Does this align with my joy?"

One of my clients found that his purpose lay in being a father. He had wanted a family from the time he was a small child and had always sought out good jobs so that he could be a strong provider.

Once he met his wife and they had children, his purpose was confirmed. There was nothing in life that made him happier than his children. Discovering this led him and his wife to swap roles within the family. He became a stay-at-home father, and she took over the role of breadwinner. They are much happier now that they are both in positions that allow them to live out their own purpose and happiness.

If you're living a purpose that doesn't bring you joy, it's not your true purpose.

What Brings You Joy?

One of the statements that I hear most often from clients is that they don't know what their life purpose is; they are unsure of what brings them true joy. It can be overwhelming to think about this without the help of a guide, which is exactly why I'm here to help you!

One of my favorite ways to help people discover their true purpose is to ask them to picture themselves when they were between the ages of 7 and 12 years old. What got your heart racing then? What really piqued your interest? Climbing trees? Playing with a chemistry set? Making crafts? Exploring your neighborhood?

It's often in these memories that we find our true selves and

HONING OUR DESIRES

According to modern science, the big bang theory—the theory behind the creation of our Universe—hinges on the idea that the Universe is constantly expanding. Every day, every second, the Universe gets a little bit bigger, expanding out into the far reaches of space, and also within ourselves. This expansion creates a massive amount of potential energy that we can utilize in our transformation and development. Thinking deeply about our desires helps us identify our priorities. We can then refocus the different parts of our lives to be aligned with these priorities.

One thing to be mindful of is the difference between society-driven desires (things you feel you *should* do) and your true inner desires (things you feel internally *guided* to do in order to be happy). True desires, the ones that are unspoiled by the false values society forces on us, are less about thinking and more about feeling. Wanting to be a singer because of fame and money is different from being guided to sing simply because it makes you happy to sing, and knowing that if you're not singing, you're not happy.

So many people find themselves chasing after what they want or think they want, instead of what they really need. The key is to realign our focus with our true desires and to take a step back so we can see where those desires come from.

in turn, our true happiness. People change over time, but the things that make us truly happy seem to simply change form— at heart, it's still the same basic idea that makes us happy. If playing with a chemistry set brought you happiness and excitement, perhaps you enjoy discovering new things and doing research. It doesn't have to be science-related; it may be the act of discovery that intrigues you.

I will never forget meeting Ella. Ella was a client of mine who was desperately seeking guidance when we connected a couple of years ago. She had just graduated college and had taken whatever job she could, because her loans were coming due soon. She was terrified about her student debt and, at the time, the economy was in a downward spiral. Ella didn't know how she was going to pay off her debt when she hadn't been successful in acquiring a job in her field, and the job she did have didn't pay very much. Her family didn't have much to spare financially, and she felt that asking them for assistance was not an option she wanted to explore.

Ella had completed a degree in business because that is what her family wanted for her, and she didn't want to disagree or disappoint them. Ella shared with me that she had always done what her family wanted—and for good reason, as they wanted what was best for her. She threw herself into her academics and did reasonably well, but she wasn't passionate about her selected field of study. After four years of business school, she graduated and went out into the world. She didn't want to work in an office and had no idea what else to do with a business degree. When I asked her what *she* wanted to do, she really didn't know.

Together, we worked through several processes trying to figure out what actually made her happy. After a couple of sessions together, she revealed a love for crafting. Whenever she was stressed about a final exam or worried about a presentation, she would knit, crochet, or even make jewelry. Her grandmother had taught her how to craft when she was a young girl, and doing these things always reminded her of her grandmother, which helped her to calm down, enabling her to tackle the stressful situation. This huge breakthrough allowed us to put together a plan that would both make her family proud and allow her to focus on her own happiness.

Within a couple of months of our first session, Ella had opened an online Etsy shop and was running her own business selling her handmade goods. She was so happy to be able to combine her education and her passion. She found what made her happy and turned it into her full-time job. When Ella first made her joy list, she hadn't even considered including crafting, but once she was going through several processes a day, and really trying to focus on what made her happy and what she was grateful for, she found it.

Tap into your memories of joy and ponder them for a while. Explore them and discover what they reveal about your own personal truths.

Joy needs to be our number one priority. We need to rest in and trust the wisdom and knowing of our deepest desires.

The Mind and Prosperity

Throughout our evolution as a species, the human brain has become the perfect observer.

We can use our five senses to deduce almost everything about our environment, which likely evolved as a way to protect us from predators. It is also a fine-tuning of the problem-solving skills we already had. Our minds are excellent observers, and we can further our journey to prosperity by allowing the mind to fulfill that role and that role alone. Our five senses were honed through survival and fear. We learn to do things, or not do them, because it helps our survival in one way or another.

In some regards, the brain is very similar to a three-year-old child. A three-year-old doesn't know not to touch the hot stove until she uses her senses to deduce that touching it hurts, and threatens her health or survival. Instead of allowing the three-year-old child to be in control of our feelings and actions, we need to allow our spirit to lead the way.

As human beings in the modern world, we have a habit of pushing ourselves too hard, of putting too much pressure on the brain to be perfect, to succeed, to have all the answers, even while we are learning something new. Would you tell a three-year-old that she was unintelligent because she didn't grasp a new idea immediately, and because of that, he was incapable of succeeding? No, of course not! She is just a child, and she doesn't know any better.

Yet this is exactly what we do to our own minds, and it's just as unfair.

We need to go easier on the mind, to be more caring and less judgmental. Our mind doesn't know any better. The harder we push, the more it resists—just like a toddler will. If you push and push a toddler into doing what you want him or her to do, you will likely end up with an unhappy, tantrum-throwing child. If you encourage, guide, and show a toddler what you want and why, the child is far more likely to understand and go along.

We need to be patient with our minds and give them time to adjust to and consider new ideas. If we allow our spirit, our intuition, to lead the mind, to guide it gently through decisions and desires, we have a greater chance of being on task and on purpose than if we drag our mind kicking and screaming into a whole new way of looking at things.

Transcending Fear

As we evolve, we develop new skills to overcome fear. It's my honor to be able to share with you another way to deal with and move through the emotion of fear with more ease than what most people experience.

The idea of fear itself can be challenging. Even just thinking about the things we fear can cause our heart rate to spike and our breath to quicken. Many people who experience anxiety can relate to the immediate adrenaline rush that can come from an upcoming deadline.

What if I were to tell you that fear isn't bad or good—that it's just the mind (our inner 3-year-old) trying to protect itself from something it's unfamiliar with?

Well, that's exactly what fear is. We can better understand fear when we choose to think less and feel more. It seems kind of backward, right? But by thinking less and letting our intuition and feelings guide us more often, we can *observe* the fear instead of reacting to it.

Fear, whether of failure or success, is just an emotion. It's not rooted in reality. If you're afraid of something and you succeed at it anyway, nothing has really changed, except your perception of yourself.

A number of authors and teachers, such as Lissa Rankin, have written about how fear affects us and holds us back in life. There seem to be four main types of fear that most people experience: fear of failure, fear of success, fear of the unknown, and fear of losing something. None of these can hold their own outside of our minds once we step outside of our thinking and realize that there is no such thing as the "unknown." We all come from universal energy. We all come from the stars. What we consider to be the "unknown" is simply energy the mind has forgotten about.

Furthermore, even when we experience fear and don't succeed, failure isn't the end. If you fail to win your game, baseball doesn't stop playing! "Failure" is simply feedback that enables us to discover an experience we don't want more of. Success is feedback that helps us discover which experiences we *do* want more of. That's all it is!

Doesn't this simple shift in perspective feel so much better than the pressure and fear people carry around about success and failure?

What you refer to as failure doesn't make you less of a person just because you experienced it. Creating what you *don't* want actually blesses you with the awareness of what you *do* want to create in life.

Trusting in the Universe eliminates any need for fear. If you can put your trust in the Universe and follow your intuition, you are well on your way to a fear-free, prosperity-filled life!

Developing Intuition

Some of my more analytical readers—those who tend to think in logical steps and focus more on reasoning than on feeling— may have a bit of an awakening here, so bear with me. The key to developing our intuition is to *think less and feel more*.

This allows us to get in touch with and trust our spirit, and to make decisions that the mind might not be capable of making. This doesn't mean we've stopped thinking, but rather that we're giving our minds and ourselves a break from constant thought, allowing us the opportunity to intuitively feel our way through our lives.

People are often confused about feelings versus emotions when I ask them to *think less and feel more*. I define an emotion as a reaction to something that stems from outside of us. When you're driving down the street and someone cuts you off, your emotion is anger or frustration at being cut off. It's an effect due to a cause. Something external has triggered an emotion.

A feeling, on the other hand, comes from our gut, without the judgment of good or bad. It speaks to our individual situation, letting us know intuitively about what is right for us. It is also a recognition that just because a particular choice is right for me, doesn't mean that it will be right for you, and vice versa. Framing questions about our desires and choices according to whether they make us feel *expansive* or *constricted* is a great way to be able to determine if something is aligned with our highest path.

Feeling expansive when you consider an idea is an indicator that it is something that makes you feel more connected to who you are. Feeling constricted about something indicates that the idea doesn't have enough connection to your true self. If you're feeling constricted about something, you might be having agitated or frustrated emotions surrounding that idea. It may simply mean that as far as that idea goes, you're not on your path and need to realign.

It doesn't mean that everyone will feel that way in that same situation. Everyone has his or her own path and different situations make people feel things differently—bungee jumping isn't for everyone!

The Power of Fluidity

When we feel instead of think our way through our lives, we open ourselves up to a much greater flow of energy from the Universe.

The fluidity that our intuitive feelings create within us generates a field of opportunity around us. We are significantly more flexible and aware of change when we don't let our minds lead. When we are not bogged down with sensory input and subconsciously worried about survival, we're better able to make decisions and judge if our actions are in alignment with our desires. If they are—if we are actively pursuing our happiness—then we can rest assured that we're on target.

The feeling of fluidity occurs when you allow yourself to take in what the Universe is giving you, which creates a situation where everything comes together like well-fitted puzzle pieces. You have all had the experience of just stepping into a situation where nothing stands in the way of your goal, and the pieces of what you've worked toward come together perfectly. That is the essence of fluidity. If you allow your feelings—your intuition—that power, you are better situated to receive more of those auspicious circumstances. Being in the flow opens you up to a more prosperous reality.

I once worked with a client, Calvin, who came to me expressing feelings and thoughts of being stuck in his life. He wasn't particularly happy or unhappy with his job or his family; he just felt that he could have more. Calvin was a very strict A-to-B person. He had followed his five-year plan and pulled it off by working really hard . . . but he wasn't fulfilled. He wanted more out of life. He wanted to be able to open himself up to more opportunities, but he didn't know how to start.

We worked together for a couple of months on pursuing

fluidity and connection to the Universe. We talked through his hesitations, emotions, and thoughts. Once he was able to put his mind aside and let the Universe lead and take control, he was far better able to flow through his life and feel like he was fully living it.

He contacted me one day on his lunch break, very excited, and told me about a new position that had opened up at his work. Calvin had applied for it with a positive energy but hadn't really thought much about it until he was called back for an interview. He was calling me after the interview to tell me that he had successfully acquired the job. Not only was there a significant pay raise, but additionally, he and his family were moving back to his wife's hometown where the majority of her family still lived.

He was thrilled that not only would they have a bigger support network in their new location, but that he would also be better able to provide for his family. Calvin informed me that during the interview one of his bosses had commented that he hadn't thought Calvin was the right person for the job until recently, when he seemed to be more able to relax and go with the flow of the office.

Calvin's initial moment of intuition guiding him to open himself up to new opportunities had triggered an entire series of events that led him to a happier, more stable, and more desirable situation, both at work and at home.

Calvin's story is a perfect illustration of what happens when you pursue your desires by thinking less and feeling more.

Qualities, Not Specifics

People aren't always sure about what makes them happy. Even after remembering what made them joyful during childhood and trying to focus more on what actively makes them happy now in their daily life, this can still be a bit of a challenge for some people.

One trick I've learned is to focus on the *qualities* that make you happy, the essence of what you enjoy. Looking at the qualities instead of the specifics of your desires can quickly bring to light what you'd like to experience more of.

For example, if your desire is to have a million dollars, that's a specific form. Asking yourself, "What does a million dollars provide me with?" can open your eyes to the qualities that you're searching for. In this case, a million dollars might provide you with the qualities of security, flexibility, or freedom of choice. Examining the qualities of what we want—and our reasons for wanting them—opens us up to be more available to the blessings coming our way, because we're not so fixated on the specific what, where, when, and how of our desires.

When we focus on the overall goal instead of the specifics, we successfully open ourselves up to more opportunities, because we aren't bogged down by a narrow set of outer circumstances. Focusing on qualities allows us the freedom to pursue the full essence of what we want, not just limited forms of it.

Many of my clients have indicated that this goes against many common teachings that focus on picturing the literal, specific goal in mind. That method can definitely have benefits, especially if you're a person who needs a specific goal in order to get yourself moving. But once you've gained that momentum, losing the specifics and focusing on the qualities creates openings for a broader range of creative solutions.

PROSPERITY PROCESSES:

FINDING YOUR HAPPINESS

The following processes will help you to refocus your energy and apply it to creating a more prosperous frame of mind.

As I noted earlier, it takes 21 days to break a habit and 28 days to establish a new one. Keep this in mind when you're starting your prosperity processes. If we commit to trying each new process for 28 days, we should be able to break ourselves out of the old habits and convert that energy into support for our new habit. Don't be too hard on yourself, but stick with it, and remember to push through when you feel yourself resisting these changes.

Sometimes when we try to begin a new habit, we can find ourselves resisting. This resistance is our mind throwing a temper tantrum, trying to get us to stay on the same old familiar track. When we meet resistance within ourselves over any of these processes, that is a strong indicator that those are the processes that will benefit us the most.

Resistance to change is feedback that a huge breakthrough or a shift in perception is about to occur. So instead of feeling defeated when resistance comes up, we can actually use it to motivate us to move through the process, because now we know something amazing awaits us on the other side.

The Joy List

This exercise will help you to realize and focus on the things in life that bring you happiness and joy. For this process, I'll need you to get a piece of paper and a pen or pencil.

STEP 1: At the top of the page, title your list "The Joy List" or "Things That Make My Heart Sing."

STEP 2: Take a moment to reflect on some of the things in your life that make you happy. This might mean thinking back to when you were a kid, when you loved to climb trees. It might be enjoying the perfect cup of hot cocoa.

STEP 3: Write those things down.

STEP 4: Start to implement one, if not more, of the items on this list in your daily life. If you like to read, maybe you can set aside 30 minutes every day to enjoy reading a good book.

This list doesn't have to be created in one sitting. It is a living, breathing document. You can add and subtract items from it as you travel through your journey. The list also doesn't have to be exclusive to your work or personal life—it can contain both or just one. You could have multiple lists, as long as the items on them make you truly happy.

Mantras

When we think of happiness, we think of having peace of mind and heart, of healing whatever troubles us, of fulfilling our dreams. There are different ways of working with energy, so that we are able to experience healing, have a peaceful outlook on life, and birth our desires into the outer world.

Mantras are sacred phrases and chants that have been used for thousands of years by millions of people around the world, with the intention of manifesting their deepest and truest desires.

The energy in these words and phrases helps to put our intentions out into the world, bringing them back to us. Each word carries a specific vibration. These vibrations, coupled with clear intention and consistent repetition, will help anchor your ideas and desires into physical form.

Mantras are a powerful tool for transformation, healing, and prosperity. I've worked with mantras for many years and attribute much of my prosperity to them. They are spoken in the ancient language of Sanskrit, which is a language based first on sounds that carry certain energy vibrations and second on actual meanings.

I learned about mantras when I first moved to Los Angeles. Having come from a small town, the city was quite overwhelming to the senses in every way. After a few weeks of being in Los Angeles, I mentioned to a new friend I had made how overwhelmed I was feeling with my recent move. Without hesitation, she asked if I had ever worked with mantras. At first, I thought she was talking about positive affirmations. However, she quickly enlightened me that the mantras she was referring to were the sacred mantras used for thousands of years in the Far East. My new friend had such a strong conviction that these mantras could help me better cope with my move to Los Angeles that I was beyond eager to start working with them.

I went home that day and casually began working with the mantras my friend suggested for me. Over the coming days, I started to feel a subtle vibrational shift within me that allowed me to feel calmer and less fearful. A few weeks later, I was feeling empowered and completely comfortable living in a large new city. That prompted me to learn more about the array of mantras available and the benefits they can have.

With each mantra I used, I kept experiencing amazing results. Whether it was creating more financial abundance, well-being, or everything in between, it felt as though opportunities were opening up for me left and right, creating more of my desired reality.

There are many powerful mantras that you can start working with to shift your energy and your conscious and subconscious beliefs. The key to using mantras is to be very disciplined and consistent by saying them every day. Before I start chanting a mantra, I reflect on how many people before me have said these words with the same intention, adding increasing levels of energy to these phrases over time. I also like to express gratitude to the Universe for the blessings I have already received and that are still on their way, as a direct result of chanting the mantras.

I repeat each mantra 108 times, using a mala mantra necklace with 108 beads to help me keep count. Although repeating a mantra a specific amount of times isn't necessary, the number 108 is significant for many reasons. For one, about 7,000 years ago in ancient India, learned people were able to correctly calculate that the distance from the earth to the sun was equal to the diameter of the sun times 108, and that the distance from the earth to the moon was equal to the diameter of the moon times 108. There are also 54 letters in the Sanskrit alphabet, each with a masculine and feminine aspect (*Shiva* and *Shakti*)—54 times 2 equals 108.

You can repeat a mantra as many times as you need to, to help yourself feel guided. But it is a good idea to spend at least 30 seconds on each mantra.

STEP 1: Find yourself a nice, quiet place to sit and get comfortable.

STEP 2: Contemplate how many people before you have said these mantras with the same intention as you are about to express.

STEP 3: Repeat the following mantras:

- **Om gum ganapataye namaha** (Om guhm guh-nuh-puh-tuh-yay nah-mah-hah): Clears obstacles to a happy, healthy, prosperous life.

- **Om shreem maha l'akshmye namaha** (Om shr-eem mah-hah lahk-shmee-yay nah-mah-hah): Attracts prosperity in all areas of life.

- **Om breez namaha** (Om brah-zee nah-mah-hah): Attracts good fortune and abundance.

If you have questions about how to pronounce these mantras, you're not alone. There are dozens of helpful, magical videos on YouTube that can walk you through the pronunciations.

Sometimes all we need is to be able to hear someone else pronounce a mantra before we can understand how to do it ourselves. Simply do a search on YouTube by the name of the mantra, and you will find plenty of options to choose from!

The Quality List

Making a Quality List can help us to focus on what we would like more of in our lives. By looking at the bigger picture of our desires—the root of our desires—we can better judge what will help us to achieve them. A Quality List will help us to refocus our energy on the inside, so we are better able to attract the right kind of energy on the outside.

STEP 1: Gather a couple of pieces of paper and a pen or pencil. Find somewhere to sit where you won't be disturbed.

STEP 2: Write a list of qualities you want to embody— qualities your life could use more of, such as stability, freedom, happiness, flexibility, etc.

STEP 3: Write out a short list of things that you would like in your life, such as a relationship, more money, or a vacation.

STEP 4: With those things in mind, ask yourself, "What quality does _____ provide for me?" and write down the answers. For instance, if you're asking for a relationship, it might provide comfort, affection, intimacy, and friendship.

STEP 5: Looking at the list of qualities that you've determined, ask yourself, "Where does my life already exhibit these qualities?" Example: Just because you aren't in a romantic relationship right now doesn't mean that your life is lacking in love and support. Write down some of the positive aspects of your nonromantic relationships and the gifts that you are already receiving from them.

During this process, focus on expansive, not constricting thought. Ask what you can do to promote these qualities and where they are already working in your life. Concentrate on what does exist, not on what doesn't.

Focusing on the inner qualities we want, instead of the outer specifics, opens us up to blessings beyond anything we could have ever imagined for ourselves.

Summary

Together, prosperity and happiness can help to pave the way to a better life. Taking charge of how we feel and think can help to eliminate fear, help us focus on what matters to us, and allow us to work on achieving our personal and professional goals.

Happiness is about so much more than the contents of our bank account or how many friends we have. Happiness is being happy with ourselves and the journey we are on. Prosperity is about what we achieve and how we see the world.

We are enough. We are never lacking. We always have the capacity to receive more. Once we have brought these concepts into our lives, we're ready to open ourselves up to the idea of circulation and how that affects our energies.

Embracing Circulation

W hat I'm about share with you in this chapter may radically change your experience of prosperity on a permanent basis.

My own radical shift in this area began when I took a chance on myself by leaving a well-paying job in the corporate world. I was at a point where I knew I wanted a change but didn't know how to enact it. Like many creative types, I wasn't feeling fulfilled sitting in a cubicle all day long. My life wasn't making me happy, and I needed a change. Living for the weekends wasn't the way I wanted to spend the rest of my life.

But in my attempt to pursue my dreams, I struggled. I just didn't have the awareness and knowledge of how to open myself up to the Universe so I could receive its abundant gifts.

One of the fundamental principles of physics is the law of conservation of energy; energy cannot be created or destroyed, only converted to a different form. This also holds true for our personal energies. If we engage in lower vibrational thoughts about something, we will draw experiences into our lives that match those lower vibrational thoughts. This also applies to the life-enhancing thoughts we choose to engage in. These are the thoughts that lead us to greater expansion and a more positive life experience. Many people call this karma, the idea that what we put out into the world comes back to us.

When I left my corporate job, I held the belief that pursuing my passions and making a good living while doing it might not be in the cards for me. I thought that even if it did happen, it would be difficult to achieve.

I was so stuck on this idea of "success equals struggle" that I forgot all about my seventh-grade science fair project.

Shifting Your Mindset

When I was in seventh grade, I wanted to explore whether music had an effect on plants. I raised two identical plants and gave them the exact same amounts of water, fertilizer, and sunlight. The only difference was that one plant listened to classical music for hours each day, while the other listened to aggressive heavy metal.

By the end of the experiment six weeks later, the plant listening to classical music was thriving, beautiful, and healthy. The plant listening to the heavy metal every day had withered and suffered. It looked nothing like the plant exposed to classical music. The heavy metal plant wasn't happy; it told me that in its struggle to survive.

This taught me that the energies we surround ourselves with have an effect on how we think and behave. Everything we do is about the giving and receiving of energies. It's a constant give and take between the Universe and everything that lives inside of it.

What is the purpose of my sharing this story with you? I realized that the plants, even though they seemed to be just objects in front of me, were still live beings. Plants are living, breathing entities that share the world with us. Even though those plants didn't have personalities, they still communicated their needs. Money is the same way. In our everyday lives, money is the physical aspect of the energy of abundance. And like all energy, it embodies the principle of circulation.

In its energetic form, money is a living, breathing being.

While working on my relationship with money, I went through a deeply reflective period that almost felt like I was in mourning. I looked at money as if it were not spiritual. I saw it as a bad, problem-causing obstacle.

I have come to learn that this is simply not true. I was projecting my negative ideas onto money. Money is trying to serve people. As I moved through this period, I started to feel gratitude and compassion for money. Can you imagine projecting the idea that your best friend is evil and not spiritual? That you have to fight for the friendship—that it's a struggle to be around them? This is what we do to money!

Once I realized this, I felt disappointed in myself. I was sad that I had been putting all of these negative projections onto this entity that simply wanted to fulfill its purpose of being a means of giving and receiving.

Remembering the music experiment taught me an awareness that I'd never had before. I realized that plants, rocks, and Nature as a whole, are all energy—and that money is also energy. The tangible items that we think of as money are really just a symbol of the living, breathing entity that is the energy of money and abundance.

Once I remembered this, it changed everything for me.

Money is alive; it's not just a lifeless object. It's the living energy behind the symbol that is currency and the collective energy of circulation. I'd assumed that it was lifeless and lacking in energy, because I hadn't known any better. I hadn't been taught differently. I had been making it all about myself and not taking into account how money felt about the negative beliefs I held about it. This new awareness allowed me to have a new kind of relationship with money.

What Is Money?

Money's only purpose is to bless all those it meets. That's it! That is all it is.

Money is the physical embodiment of the energies of giving and receiving: the embodiment of circulation. But how often have we actually thought about giving back to the actual energy of money itself?

When we start to bless, support, and be of service to money, it will return to us in manifold ways. Before we had physical cash or coins, we had the barter system—trading your bushel of hay for my goat. It was a system of equal trade and sharing, for the betterment of everyone. This is all money wants to be—a positive representation of the relationships between people.

Money symbolizes sharing, growth, reciprocity, and strength. Yet money is so frowned upon in our society. Everyone chases after it without giving any thought to the energy of money itself. People act as if money exists in limited quantities, that it has to be rationed because there isn't enough to go around.

This couldn't be further from the truth.

There is an *infinite* amount of money in this world. There is so much wealth waiting to be shared. When we shift the way we view and treat money, our experience with it will completely transform for the better. This ties into the Principle of Reciprocity, which is simply that for every energetic "action"—for every bit of energy we put out—the Universe sends us an equal and opposite reaction or give-back. This is a natural process in the Universe: what we put out is what we receive back.

Dissolving Lack Mentality

When I first started to take on clients, I intended nothing more than to work on a one-to-one basis. I thought I might see three or four clients a day and be able to maintain my lifestyle and my business that way. I felt that I didn't need much to be happy, just enough to get by.

This narrow image of what was possible for my work and income was due, in part, to my lack mentality. I wasn't focusing on how much I had to give, just on how little I was getting in return. But the more I focused on how much I could give, the more I received.

This was never clearer than when the organizer of one of the largest mind-body-spirit conferences asked me to speak at her summit. After reflecting upon the offer, I accepted, because there was no way I was going to turn down such a huge opportunity to share my core message of uplifting and empowering others to live their full potential.

I have no idea how they found me, but I'm so glad they did, because speaking at that summit helped me see my life work in far more expansive ways. That one summit generated enough cash flow to set up my new business for a year. It also led me to many other opportunities that completely shifted me out of the limitations I had created for myself on my life path.

In that moment, I saw that I had created my own windfall.

The money wasn't coming to me because I was selfish or because I worked harder than everyone else—though I did work hard.

The money came to me because of how I treated it *before* it arrived.

I gave up my lack mentality so that I could open myself up to new and exciting opportunities. By letting the Universe and its energy into my life, by allowing my intuitive feelings to lead me to my desires, I was able to generate prosperity in previously unexpected ways.

Rebalancing Debt

Debt is simply an imbalance between giving and receiving, an imbalance in circulation.

Getting out of debt becomes much easier to do once we shift the energy involved from taking to giving. Once we ask how we can be of service to money and to one another, we allow for greater opportunities. If we take too much, we experience debt. It's only by giving of ourselves and our time and energy that we can give back and rebalance circulation.

I once had a powerful experience with one of my clients, Anna. When she first came to work with me, she was headed toward bankruptcy. She was about to lose her house, her car, and her credit rating, and her once-successful relationship was teetering on the brink of failure.

Anna and I began integrating into her life many of the concepts provided in this book. Then about one month after our first session, I received a joyous call from Anna. She explained that many years ago, she'd had the opportunity to meet a distant cousin at a family reunion. During the gathering she had noticed that many of her relatives were gossiping and distanc-

the change in behavior and thought that it would make him a good team leader. If he could handle the stress as a contractor, the stress of managing the team wouldn't be a deal breaker.

By being of service, both by volunteering in his community and by taking days off solely to spend time with his family, he was better able to pursue his own prosperity and happiness.

Service doesn't have to mean donating money to a cause or volunteering at a soup kitchen—though these are acts of service. Being of service also means giving of yourself, your time, your talents, and yes, your energy. You might go out and volunteer in your community, or you might simply help your elderly neighbor go grocery shopping.

Giving and being of service isn't necessarily a physical giving either, such as raking your neighbor's leaves while you are doing your own. It could also mean spending 20 minutes on the phone with your mother or grandmother. Even when we feel like we have nothing, when we think we're lacking energy, there is always something that we can give.

When we focus on giving our time, energy, and gifts, we are also giving ourselves permission to step out of our heads. We can move out of the solitary mindset of *me, me, me* and into prosperity consciousness—abundance consciousness. If we can be of service to our community with our time, talents, and love, we will find ourselves blessed many times over.

Giving promotes prosperity, even when the gift isn't monetary. Giving something to others helps us move out of a lack mentality and toward a more prosperous existence.

Strengthening Our Giving-and-Receiving Muscles

When working toward prosperity, it's important to remember that receiving is just as important as giving. If you find yourself in a position where you're giving more than you're receiving, you may not be in alignment with your path. You might want to consider making some adjustments.

One of the best situations I've come across for strengthening your receiving muscles is going out for a meal with a client, coworker, or friend. After you've had your meal and discussed your work, the projects you're creating together, and family, the bill arrives.

Traditionally, in many cultures, it's polite for both parties to offer to pay. Then whoever insists the most, saying, "Oh no, please—let me grab the check," is the one who pays. It's often the case that people want to pick up the check because they want to be the one giving and providing for their client, colleague, or friend. But it can bring about a big change in your thinking to allow the other person to pay, with no more than a polite refusal at first.

One thing that helped me to overcome my need to give in this situation was changing my perspective. Instead of focusing on giving, I altered my thinking to be able to honor the act of receiving. I've been known to say, "I'm going to honor you by accepting your gift," treating the meal as a gift and being thankful for it.

If there's one thing a client taught me, it's that this isn't always so easy. It can be difficult for people to learn to accept gifts, especially without feeling as if they have to reciprocate. It is important to learn how to receive, as well as to give. A friend of mine had a very hard time with this when she started her new job. Kelly had just taken a new sales position at her company and really wanted to impress her bosses and the clients she'd inherited from the previous head of sales. She was given an expense budget to work with for client dinners and lunches, but she quickly blew it. She wanted to make all of her clients feel pampered and taken care of, in the hopes that she would not only look good, but also make her employer happy and more comfortable with her taking over the department.

Her insecurity caused some problems with her boss and finance team. She was told that she couldn't continue as she had been, or she would lose her job. The budget didn't support the kind of outings she was taking her clients on. She called me for help, in tears after the meeting, and asked what I thought she should do. Kelly is a brilliant woman and an excellent salesperson, but she was terrified of not succeeding. She didn't want to look powerless in front of her clients by allowing them to pay for anything while they were in town visiting her.

I raised the concept that by refusing to allow her clients, or even potential clients, to pick up the bill occasionally or buy their own tickets to a show, she was denying them the chance to give her something in return for what she does. I reminded her that receiving is just as important as giving and that people need to allow themselves to be comfortable in both positions. Kelly took these suggestions onboard, and when I last heard from her, she had settled into the new position and was thriving, acquiring new clients as well as maintaining the inherited client database, without blowing her budget. She graciously allowed clients to pick up the tab on occasions, while still preserving strong professional relationships. This validated for her that the mutual act of giving and receiving was in fact healthier than her previous mindset of constantly giving.

When you allow someone else to pick up the tab, you're accepting their gift and making them feel good. Those moments are just as important as when you're the one paying the bill. The key is balance. If a client insists, don't overpower them; accept their gift and thank them graciously. Next time, you can insist on treating them.

Allowing someone else the position of giving and providing can be just as empowering for you as the recipient, as it is when you are the provider. It's important to make room in your personal life, and in your business or career, for both giving *and* receiving.

Generosity

For many years, I've studied and observed well-known prosperous people to see what beliefs and ideas they had in common. I desired to understand what formula they were using that seemed to connect all the dots for them, and that had helped them create such a joyfully abundant and fulfilling reality.

What I found was absolutely amazing and felt almost too simple! I discovered that one of the most powerful ingredients these prosperous people had in common, and worked with daily, was generosity. Whether or not they'd done it intentionally, some of the most prosperous, wealthy, and admired people in the world, such as Oprah Winfrey and Richard Branson, had long ago discovered the importance of giving as a part of creating their own abundance. When I say they were working with generosity, I don't mean they gave once a year to their favorite charity. I mean they were living and breathing generosity on a daily basis. It seems to be a very high priority for them to express generosity as often as possible. Why was that? I wondered.

In fact, generosity seems to be part of living abundantly in the fullest sense—which includes good health, peace of mind, fulfilling relationships—and not just owning "stuff" as Richard Branson calls it. If you look around, you'll find that those who are not only amazingly wealthy but also living very fulfilling lives have invested very deeply in the idea of generosity, not just as something that would help them prosper. They realized that we get back whatever we give in this life. They also see generosity as a way of being, as a life philosophy and spiritual practice.

Let's look at Richard Branson's life for a moment. He started out as an entrepreneur while he was still in his teens. He has said that he wasn't trying to make money or become famous, but that he "wanted to change the world." He left school at 15 to start *Student* magazine, to campaign against the Vietnam War. He then branched out into selling records, creating the Virgin record label and Virgin record stores. By age 28, he'd bought a private island in the Caribbean. Since the 1970s, he's launched one business after another—Virgin Atlantic Airways, Virgin Trains, Virgin Mobile. The Virgin Group now consists of more than 400 businesses, including space travel company Virgin Galactic.[1]

Branson had learned early on about generosity. He had started his magazine with a handful of coins he found in a public phone booth at school, but it was his mother's donation of £300 that really got things rolling, and he has never forgotten that. He says that he "always wanted the opportunity to make a difference" and that "a successful entrepreneur's mission

1   Rebecca Burn-Callander, "Exclusive Interview: Sir Richard Branson,"
    Vision magazine, January 2014, http://vision.ae/focus/exclusive_interview_
    sir_richard_branson.

should be about making people's lives better." The wealthier
Branson became, the more his outlook broadened. He looked
to see how he could give back, and who he could encourage
and inspire. In the late 1990s, he and musician Peter Gabriel
worked with Nelson Mandela to create the Elders, a group of
leaders from around the world, such as Jimmy Carter, Mary
Robinson, and Archbishop Tutu, who work to create peaceful
resolutions to conflicts around the world.[2]

In 1999, Branson became a founding sponsor of the International Centre for Missing & Exploited Children.[3] He also
launched Virgin Startup, which has provided more than $1 million in loans to more than 100 businesses created by young
entrepreneurs throughout the United Kingdom. He created
the Branson School of Entrepreneurship in South Africa in
2005, partnering his nonprofit Virgin Unite with a program
created by a Johannesburg entrepreneur, to support startups
and small businesses with skills, loans, and mentoring—and he
is one of the mentors. In 2010, he founded Enterprise Zimbabwe with the Nduna Foundation and Humanity United.

Branson has given of himself, as well as his money. He often
lends his name or gives time to a peace campaign or another
nonprofit cause. He hosts environmental gatherings about
global warming on his island, with other entrepreneurs, media
people, and world leaders. In May 2009, Branson took over
Mia Farrow's hunger strike for three days to protest the Sudanese government ordering aid groups to leave Darfur. Branson
has said that life has to be about more than making money. In

---

2 Rebecca Burn-Callander, "Exclusive Interview: Sir Richard Branson."
3 Rebecca Burn-Callander, "Exclusive Interview: Sir Richard Branson."

2013, Branson announced that he and his wife would be donating half of their $5 billion personal fortune to charity, to help to create a "healthy, equitable and peaceful world for future generations to enjoy."[4]

It's hard to imagine Branson having done so well financially without having given so much to so many. I believe that he discovered early on that when you give to others, you are saying to yourself, the world, and the Universe, "I have plenty. I have more than I need. Money is no problem for me. I'm doing great, and I would like to give back." That reality is then reflected back to you, for as long as you keep giving. Even when you think you have little or nothing to spare, the act of giving itself shifts you from feeling that you "need more money," which is an energy that actually repels abundance. It lifts you out of that reality and into the feeling of having more than enough. Money loves the feeling of prosperity, and as you attain that feeling by being generous, money and other forms of abundance will respond by pouring into your life all the more.

Oprah Winfrey is another very famous self-made billionaire, though unlike Branson, she was not born into a privileged life. But when she was small, she lived with her grandmother, who gave the two-and-a-half-year-old Oprah the great gift of early reading lessons. Another gift was that she was allowed to speak in church, reciting poetry and bible verses beginning at age two and a half.

As most people know, Oprah's life was very hard when she was growing up. Her mother worked long hours as a maid and

4 Don Mackay, "Sir Richard Branson to Give Away Half His Fortune to Charity," *Mirror* online, accessed June 29, 2015, http://www.mirror.co.uk/news/uk-news/sir-richard-branson-give-away-1721394.

was rarely home. Oprah was sexually abused starting at age nine by several male family members, until she ran away at age 14. Yet the generosity of others, and her own courage, sustained her. As a young girl she received another gift when she read the novel *I Know Why the Caged Bird Sings* by Maya Angelou and immediately connected with that inspiring story. In her mid-teens, she moved back in with her father, who gave her strict guidelines on how to behave and insisted that she read one book a week, write a book report on it, and learn five new vocabulary words each day. A teacher who noted Oprah's talents for writing and speaking helped her get into a much better high school than she had been headed for, another act of kindness she would later pass on to others.

After winning a beauty contest when she was 17, Oprah was offered an on-air job at a Nashville radio station. She had won a full scholarship to Tennessee State University and continued working at the station during her first few years of college. She was soon hired as a reporter and news anchor for a local TV station, then became a news anchor in Baltimore, where she also co-hosted her first talk show. She moved the Chicago in 1984 to host *AM Chicago* and made that show the most popular in town in less than a year. In 1985 it was renamed *The Oprah Winfrey Show*, which was soon broadcast nationally, quickly becoming the top talk show in the country. It ran for 24 years, winning many awards and only ending in 2011, as Oprah created the Oprah Winfrey Network (OWN).

Though many people are amazed to hear of Oprah's net worth ($3 billion in 2015), they are usually more impressed by Oprah's example as someone who is extremely generous, spiritually awake, and socially aware. She has donated millions to individuals, communities, colleges, educational funds, foundations, and nonprofits.

Her three nonprofit foundations have aided projects such as The Oprah Winfrey Leadership Academy for Girls in South Africa, Rebuilding the Gulf Coast, and Free The Children, an organization that builds schools in developing countries. The Angel Network alone has raised more than $51 million for nonprofit aid programs. Oprah gives of her time, effort, and money to benefit issues such as cancer awareness and research, animal rescue, HIV and AIDS, global warming, and children's services. In 2000, her Angel Network began gifting a $100,000 Use Your Life award to individuals who have dedicated their life work to improving the lives of others.[5] Oprah has also donated to Women For Women International, Peace Over Violence, the Lower East Side Girl's Club, many colleges and educational funds, and many other charities.[6]

Shows on the OWN network often devote time to discussing causes that powerfully affect people's lives, including spiritual growth. For years Oprah has highlighted the people and organizations seeking to help those stuck in dangerous or challenging life situations. In 2013, she donated $12 million to the Smithsonian's National Museum of African American History and Culture, saying that she wished to give back to "those who paved the path for me and all who follow in their footsteps."[7]

5 "Oprah Winfrey," *Achievement*, accessed June 30, 2015, http://www. achievement.org/autodoc/page/win0bio-1.

6 "Oprah: Charity Work, Events and Causes," *Look to the Stars*, accessed June 29, 2015, https://www.looktothestars.org/celebrity/oprah.

7 "Oprah Winfrey Donates $12 Million to Smithsonian," *The Washington Post* online, June 11, 2013, http://www.washingtonpost.com/entertainment/ museums/oprah-winfrey-donates-12-million-to-smithsonian/2013/06/11/3fe63b4a-d20c-11e2-a73e-826d299ff459_story.html.

Oprah has so far willed $1 billion dollars to charity.[8] Her actions have spoken more loudly and clearly than any words about generosity ever could.

Of course you and I might look at the lives of these and other amazing self-made people and decide, "That's nice, but I don't create anything on that scale!" But I think you would agree that everyone's life work is equally important. I was curious to see if giving would prosper the average person, whatever their income level or life work might be. If being generous was an actual prosperity principle, it should still prosper the giver, even if that person currently earns only a few thousand dollars a year.

I decided to adopt some of the generosity principles I had witnessed and try it myself to see what would happen. I turned it into a fun experiment—the Radical Generosity Experiment. I gave myself one month to see if anything would change in my life just because I was giving on a steady basis.

So for one month, I volunteered once a week at the local homeless shelter, cooking healthy food and spending quality time with people who were going through some financial struggles. I offered random acts of kindness in my community, such as buying groceries for the person behind me at the grocery store often, or paying for the cup of coffee for the person behind me at the coffee shop. I walked my elderly neighbor's dogs and mowed her lawn for her. I randomly tucked note cards under people's windshield wipers in parking lots, telling them how amazing they were and other encouraging words, and usually including enough money in the envelope for a nice dinner for two.

8 "Oprah: Charity Work, Events and Causes."

I also began using social media to inspire people daily. I still do this on my Facebook page, where we have Manifesting Mondays, Prayer Circle Wednesdays, and Gratitude Fridays. I invite you to go to www.facebook.com/emmanueldagher1 to participate in any of these fun and prospering weekly events. Every week since 2013, we've created a space for positive shifts to occur for people. These posts and the community that's gathered around them have helped hundreds of thousands of people around the world increase their feelings of gratitude, achieve their dreams, and lead more abundant and fulfilling lives.

After conducting this experiment and seeing the amazing changes it brought me, I began to look at generosity as a way of life, and a natural part of my day. As I personally began to dive into a whole new world of living and breathing generosity, I immediately noticed a sense of deep inner peace, joy, and contentment rise up within me, such as I had never experienced before. *Huh, well—I'll be darned!* I thought. *Could all this really be connected to generosity?*

About 11 days into my Radical Generosity Experiment, I began to notice something else. I had started to attract many of the things I had always wanted in life, including better relationships, a deep inner contentment, more clarity about what I desired to contribute to the world—and even greater opportunities to prosper!

Everything seemed to just flow to me, without my having to struggle to make it happen. It seemed like everything I needed was just naturally showing up in my life. It was almost as though it came out of thin air. Was it just a coincidence, or were things showing up as a direct result of my immersing myself in acts of generosity?

Most of us think of being generous as something we do

through monetary means. And although that is one method, there are many ways we can display generosity. We can give through the offerings of our time, energy, talents, and abilities, such as lending a helping hand as a community volunteer, as mentioned earlier in Tony's story.

At one point, I decided to pause the Radical Generosity Experiment for one week, just to see what the results of *not* giving would be. I stopped giving of my time, energy, and money, and stopped looking for ways to give or be helpful to the people I met throughout my day.

Within just three days, I noticed that things weren't flowing as easily as they had been during the experiment. I also found myself having many thoughts rooted in lack and fear. The difference this time, however, was that I could no longer stand to allow that mentality. You can believe that I *immediately* dove back into practicing generosity again, then watched to see if anything changed. And lo and behold, it did! Like clockwork, things just clicked right back into place, returning me to a place where I was thriving, not just surviving. From that day on, I made a conscious decision to live a life where being generous was at the top of my daily To-Do List.

I've found that the principle of giving out of generosity and compassion is vital for anyone's prosperity. That's as true for the average working person as it is for the famous entrepreneur. As well as witnessing this in my own life, I've also seen it happen this way for many of my clients.

I could give many examples of this. I'll share one of my favorite ones here:

Ava was a new client who had come to me after she had lost her job. She was a single mother of two young girls and was three months behind on her rent. We worked with the idea of her being more generous. Even though she thought she had nothing left to give, we found an opportunity for her to volunteer for a local elder care community. She found the work incredibly fulfilling and started to become increasingly involved in that organization.

Ava is now vice president of that community. She also travels the world speaking to single mothers who are in the same place she used to be. In addition to giving them hope and encouragement by telling her own story, she shares practical ways that they can begin moving out of the experience of lack—such as giving more of their time, money, and talents to those who need them—so that they can start experiencing greater abundance.

Being generous begins as a mindset and is then reinforced by an act. Creating the mindset first is incredibly important. The first thing we need to do when it comes to being generous is to ask ourselves whether or not we're truly ready to shift into a greater experience of prosperity in our lives.

I'll give you a little example about being ready. When I discovered the prospering power of generosity, my first instinct was to share what I had discovered with everyone I knew! What I found in sharing my newly discovered knowledge was that those who were already experiencing an abundant reality wanted to hear more about it—they were eager to implement any new tips I had to offer them about becoming more generous. On the other hand, those who were experiencing lack couldn't get me to stop talking about generosity soon enough! I was actually a bit taken aback by this, because I had thought that surely, it would be the other way around.

However, after reflecting on it for a while, I realized that many of those who are operating in a world of lack have actually become "comfortable with creating a life of discomfort." Sounds interesting and a bit strange, doesn't it? I looked at those who were living in lack and saw that it had taken a long time for them to learn how to create that kind of reality for themselves. Lack and hardship were what they knew and trusted. And in an odd sort of way, they enjoyed complaining with friends, family, and coworkers about how hard it was to pay the bills and get ahead in life.

It sounded nice to them, in theory, that they could do something productive to move out of their current experience of lack and into a more prosperous reality. But on a deeper level, they didn't know who they were *without* the lack. They had taken on that life and that belief system for so long, that they fully identified with it and didn't want to give it up.

I found that those who were still very much choosing to operate in a reality of lack instantly began to create distractions and excuses as to why they just didn't want to take any concrete action steps to turn their situation around. They were simply not ready to prosper, and I had to come to terms with that fact and realize that that was absolutely okay!

To this day, whenever a client comes to me to learn how they can create greater prosperity in their lives, the first question I ask is, Are you truly ready for change? And if so, are you willing to do the inner work necessary to create a more abundant outer world for yourself?

How do I know a client is really ready to make that shift? When I see that the discomfort they are living in now, created by the previous "lack conditioning" they had (knowingly or unknowingly) taken on, feels more uncomfortable to them than the idea of leaving their current "comfort" zone—the experience of lack that they were taught to accept as their reality. As uncomfortable as it is to be in the position of experiencing lack, it creates a ripe environment for extraordinary expansion to occur.

Having studied the actions of prosperous self-made people, conducted my own generosity experiment, and supported many people around the world in achieving greater prosperity, I've realized the incredible power of generosity. I now see it as a key component to creating a happy, fulfilling, and abundant life.

PROSPERITY PROCESSES:

EMBRACING CIRCULATION

The following processes will support you in anchoring the foundation of circulation into your daily life. They will help you to remember to shift your focus from thinking to feeling and help you to better observe how you connect with the Universe and with money itself.

These processes will also help you cement in your mind the kind of energy that money really is. They also promote kindness and generosity—two things that money adores. If one of these processes feels too challenging right now, that's okay. But come back to it soon, because the processes that we find most daunting are usually the ones we need to act on the most.

The 5-Step Money-Relationship Healing Process

Before you begin, choose something that represents money to you. It can be cash, credit cards, an expensive item, or something simple, such as receipts for things you've purchased.

Find a quiet, comfortable place to sit with your prosperity object.

STEP 1: Take the object in your right hand and place it over your heart area. Feel and think that you and money are one. Connect with the idea that everything in your experience is one with you.

STEP 2: Set the intention of apology and ask for forgiveness. You might say, "I'm so sorry, on behalf of all humankind, for how we have treated you. I'm so sorry for how *I* have treated you. Please forgive me."

STEP 3: Ask money how you can be of service to it. "What can I do to support you?" or "What can I do to help you?"

STEP 4: Express thanks and be grateful for your experience with money by saying something like, "I see you. I love you. I accept you. I bless you. Thank you for all that you have done for me."

STEP 5: Release money so it may go and help others. This allows you to show money that you have no interest in trapping it as other people do. You could say something like, "I now lovingly release you, so you can help others create their dreams."

The Quick 2-Step Money-Relationship Healing Process

Once you have mastered the longer healing process and you have started to rebuild your relationship with money, you can move on to the shorter process. Use this anytime you pay a bill, or during a 28-day cycle pattern, when you're trying to adopt a new habit or new outlook.

STEP 1: Take an object that represents money to you (credit card, cash, receipt) and hold it to your chest.

STEP 2: Repeat: "Feed the hungry, shelter the homeless, bless those you come in contact with, and return to me manyfold," until you feel satisfied that you were heard.

Some people are more comfortable being specific about "manyfold," and that's fine. If you would like to say "one-hundredfold" or even just "return to me again," that's okay too! As long as the feeling is there, that's what's important.

I have learned that the phrase that you are most *uncomfortable* with, be it "a billionfold" or "manyfold," is probably the phrase you should use. There's something blocking you there that you need to work through.

I use this shorter process with every receipt that I receive. This method helps me keep a healthy relationship with money in a way that is private and quick, while still heartfelt and true.

Carrying Cash

So many of us go through our days without any cash in our pockets. Carrying cash is one of the best ways to be not only mindful with your spending, but aware of money and its power in your life.

STEP 1: Go to the bank or ATM and take out an amount of cash that's slightly uncomfortable for you to carry around with you. For some people this might be enough for lunch, for others it might be enough to buy a large television.

STEP 2: Carry that cash around with you until you become used to carrying that much. Then, increase the amount until it feels slightly uncomfortable again.

STEP 3: Repeat step 2, increasing as much as you need to, until carrying increasingly larger amounts of cash isn't uncomfortable anymore.

Remember that the amount that is uncomfortable is the amount you should be carrying. We often find that carrying larger-than-usual amounts of cash feels uncomfortable, because we're worried about pickpockets or spending more than we should.

But by carrying larger amounts of cash, you are trusting the Universe to take care of you. You're learning to trust the Universe to provide for you, and to keep you safe when you have a lot of money.

This process can help you to get out of lack mentality. By always having cash on hand, you will be proving that the "lack" isn't real. This doesn't mean that you should drain your accounts and carry all of your money on your person or that you should necessarily spend all the cash you're carrying. But if you do find that you need it, you will have it ready, which affirms that you always have everything you need.

The Positive Affirmation Wallet

Every time I pay for something, I'm reminded of how grateful I am that I am prosperous. This isn't due to the amount of money or credit cards I have. It's because my wallet tells me I am.

Years ago when I was just starting to become actively involved in my own prosperity, I wanted a way to become more subconsciously aware of my spending and my positive associations with money. I found a plain cloth wallet and wrote prosperity affirmations on it, such as, "I am so grateful that I am now prosperous and abundant." Each affirmation was a happy thought coupled with an expression of gratitude.

I highly encourage you to do something similar. You can either buy a wallet with affirmations already on it from an independent craft seller, or you can make your own. It doesn't have to be a wallet either! You could use a tote bag or purse, as long as it's what you regularly use to hold your money.

The affirmations on the wallet or bag will create a support system for you, so that you will be reminded daily of the prosperity already in your life, and how blessed you are.

Gift Envelopes

I've often found that when I am buying into the idea that I'm lacking something I need, the only thing that can get me back on track is to give to others.

One way to give to others, while encouraging your own prosperity, is through random, anonymous gifts:

STEP 1: Get five envelopes together.

STEP 2: Place a small cash gift inside each envelope—enough to buy a coffee or a latte from your local café. Make a simple note on the front of the envelope such as "My treat!" or "Buy yourself a coffee."

STEP 3: Leave these envelopes at random places you visit throughout the day—at the grocery store, at the park, in the kitchen at work.

STEP 4: Pay attention to how the Universe blesses you in the coming hours, days, and weeks after giving these gifts.

Anonymous giving allows us to put our circulation back in balance, because we are giving without expectation of anything in return.

Summary

If you take one thing away from this book, let it be a change in your opinion of and perspective on money.

We could all help ourselves, our friends, and our families so much if we simply treated money as we would like to be treated, just as we were taught as children to treat others. You may also want to introduce these exercises to your children or grandchildren, to help them develop an understanding and positive relationship with money from an early age, which will facilitate a generational change in attitudes toward money.

Being of service to and supportive of money will not only greatly increase the positive circulation energy around us. It will also open our minds and our futures to receiving greater levels of prosperity.

Investing in Yourself

Many people come into some sort of windfall each year. A relative might leave you an inheritance, you might win a lottery, or you might receive a large bonus at work. There are dozens of ways to come into unexpected cash flow. What's important, however, isn't how much the windfall is, but what you do with it.

The first instinct for many people—especially people who don't often have a lot of money—is to spend it all on extravagant vacations and purchases. This is natural; we feel deprived of material goods that we see our friends and family having, so we aspire to be like them. We want that large flat screen TV and a cabin up north.

But what people might not think about is the importance of investing in themselves. *Investing in yourself* is the best way to work toward not only positive cash flow but also positive energy flow.

Picture yourself on an airplane. The flight attendant is

going over the safety procedures and walking you through where the exits are. She gestures at the little control panel above your head and mimes an oxygen mask coming down in the case of the cabin losing air pressure. What does she say to do? Are you to help others with their masks first, and then put your own on? Should you adjust your child's mask before fitting your own?

No. Every time the flight attendant runs through that safety instruction, she tells you to put your own mask on before assisting others. Why do you think she tells you that? *Because you can't help other people if you don't first help yourself.*

This is a huge stumbling block for the majority of clients I meet with. People love to help each other. It may seem like that isn't always true—humans seem to be constantly fighting, but when it comes down to it, we like to help one another. Helping others makes us feel good.

What we so often forget, however, is that we can't give someone a sip of water if our own cup is empty.

When I first met Joel, he would jump from topic to topic with rapid-fire energy and passion. It was intoxicating and inspiring, but obviously exhausting. He was the first to offer to refill your drink, or to order you a snack if you were hungry. He would offer you the shirt off his back if you were just a little chilly. Joel didn't have much, but he gave everything he had and more. He ran himself into the ground, and by the time I met him, he was struggling to focus and keep his energy in one place.

Joel wanted help with making his business stronger and more profitable. After talking to him for a while, we decided that our energies might be better placed if we helped him to focus on himself. His business wasn't the most profitable, but he wasn't headed toward bankruptcy either; it could wait. What couldn't wait was his health.

Joel's insistence on caring for everyone but himself had run his health into the ground. He was borderline type 2 diabetic, had recently developed an ulcer, and his anxiety levels were through the roof. Although he was more than willing to make sure that his clients had a good meal and that his family wasn't stressed out or worried, he was terrible at making sure of those things for himself.

He lived on protein bars, energy drinks, and fast food. He constantly worried about how much money he was making, how his children were doing in school, and whether his wife was happy with how little time he spent at home. After hearing about all of this, we took a few moments to center ourselves and to focus on attracting positive energies into our lives. From there, we worked on keeping Joel's cup full. We worked together to organize his time and to help him create a safe atmosphere where he felt comfortable spending time and energy on himself.

Joel loved to cook and it made him happy, but he never felt like he had the time. We planned a couple of hours a week where he could make easy, healthy foods and freeze them so that he could take them to work throughout the week. This also ensured that his family was eating well, and it eliminated one of his worries. After focusing on eating better, we tackled his anxiety. By prioritizing and delegating tasks at work, he became less anxious about running his business. This prioritization also led to increased efficiency in the office, which allowed his company to pursue more contracts and become more profitable.

Even when we are able to ignore a stranger's plight, it is

very hard to ignore the troubles of someone we know. Whether this is right or wrong is irrelevant; it's just how people tend to act. Treat yourself as you would a family member or close friend. Before we can take care of anyone else, we need to make sure that our own needs are met. When we give more than we receive, we deplete ourselves. Over time, this depletion can bring us to the point of metaphorical starvation.

The Importance of Rest

Sometimes, the best way to invest in yourself is to take a period of rest and recuperation.

It's incredibly common to push ourselves and our brains too hard and to expect too much of ourselves. When this happens, the best thing to do is to allow ourselves a sabbatical for anywhere from a couple of minutes to a couple of days or weeks. It all depends on how hard and how long you've been pushing yourself past your limits.

When you are working really hard and being productive all day, taking the occasional ten-minute break is a great idea. It allows you to regain your focus and adjust your expectations for the day. If you've been working exceedingly hard with your team on a project for months, and you finally deliver it after weeks and weeks of overtime and long, exhausting hours, you are more than entitled to a vacation to recuperate.

A client, Gabriela, came to me soon after I started working within the mind-body-spirit community. Gabriela had been running herself ragged for months, even years, trying to keep up with all of the obligations of her family, her job, and her volunteer work. She didn't want to give anything up, but couldn't figure out why nothing seemed to be working out properly in her life.

During the six months before we started working together, Gabriela was facing problems at work, her teenage son was acting out, and the animal shelter where she volunteered was thinking about closing down. She felt devastated, as if she hadn't done enough for any of them.

The first thing I noticed was that Gabriela never talked about what she did for herself. She always talked about what she did for other people and how it made *them* feel, not her. One of her first "homework" assignments was to do something that was just for her, whether it was a pedicure or relaxing in a bubble bath.

After several sessions together, Gabriela seemed genuinely more relaxed. The problems at work soon solved themselves, as she was able to calmly approach the situation with the client and work through their concerns. She worked with the animal shelter to host a fundraiser and attracted not only the money they needed, but also more volunteers. By taking time for herself, she was able to rejuvenate her mind and open herself up to talking with her son, working through the problems he was having.

If she had continued running herself ragged, she wouldn't have had the patience or ability to see other perspectives, the solutions to her problems, and the light at the end of the tunnel. Gabriela's story proves that taking time for yourself isn't selfish; it's a necessity.

Without rest and recuperation, we can't be expected to run at optimum levels or to make the best choices. The longer you go without relaxing and taking a break, the more you'll tend to think and the less you'll tend to feel.

Allow yourself moments of relaxation. It will then be so much easier to stay in alignment with your goals and visions.

Believing in Yourself

A key component of investing in yourself is believing in yourself—your gifts, your abilities, and your talents.

We so often put ourselves down and focus on what we *didn't* achieve instead of what we *did* achieve. This only lowers our emotional vibration—the level of energy that our thoughts and emotions carry. Reframing our perspective is crucial to being able to disrupt lower vibrational thoughts, such as self-criticism, negativity, resentment, fear, or sadness, and move toward higher vibrational ideas, such as gratitude, peace, joy, and fulfillment. Struggles are often a symptom of being out of alignment with our desires, but sometimes they are just a short, simple phase that we have to travel through.

When the journey takes longer than expected, or becomes increasingly difficult, that is when it's clear that we are out of alignment. That rough patch might simply be an adjustment to a new idea or way of thinking.

One adjustment that I have had to make was to continually remind myself that just because I'm not good at a task right away doesn't mean that I'll never be good at it. In Malcolm Gladwell's book *Outliers*, he comments that it takes approximately 10,000 hours to become an expert at something,[1] such as playing the guitar. That doesn't mean that you can't become proficient or even expert at something in less time than that. But on average, it takes a lot of time and dedication to become an expert at anything.

Don't let yourself start feeling down if you find that learning

---

1 Malcolm Gladwell, *Outliers: The Story of Success* (New York: Little, Brown, and Co., 2008), 47.

INVESTING IN YOUR DESIRES

If possible, you want to develop and expand not only your business or professional life, but your personal development as well.

Part of this personal development might be taking a class in something you enjoy and want to learn more about, such as signing up for a crafts group or dance class. It might be attending and participating in city council meetings, so you can better understand how your business fits into your community. Taking a course or class in a skill needed for both your personal and professional life is a great opportunity for growth. If possible, we want to develop and expand upon both our professional and our personal lives, at the same time.

Developing new skills is one aspect of this, as you need to invest in your job or business, while simultaneously helping yourself to expand and grow. Many people see professional life and personal life as two separate things, but they are really one and the same. Your business is simply an extension of who you are on a personal level. The values that you hold in business should be the same as the values you hold in your personal life.

Recognizing this will help you to stay in alignment with your true values and not become exhausted by having to juggle two different roles with opposing values.

a new skill is taking you longer than you thought it would. Be kind to yourself, and be willing to dedicate the time and effort needed to develop this new ability.

Believing in yourself is key to being able to invest in yourself—and why would you invest in something you didn't believe in?

Aligning Your Business with Your Personal Beliefs

Part of staying in alignment—keeping your outer life in balance with your true values—is remaining honest with yourself and others. A business that doesn't operate from integrity often doesn't succeed. Being transparent, open, and honest will be a reflection of your true self and will encourage others to invest in you and your desires.

For example, I've noticed that many members of the wellness community don't like having a social media platform. Some of my colleagues in the wellness and holistic health field don't feel that social media can be an extension of their personal self. They only utilize social media, if at all, as an outlet for business purposes. What they're missing is that social media can also be used to create communities.

When I first began to develop my social media platform, I was advised by several people not to put too much of myself or my energy into it, because it would take away from my practice elsewhere. I thanked them for their input, but I had a good feeling about social media, so I decided to give it a try anyway. It has worked out amazingly well for me. Without my social media connections, I wouldn't have succeeded nearly as quickly as I have.

Just last year, I was approached by Camden, who had previously advised me against expanding my social media platform. He was amazed by what I had done but worried that if he tried to do the same thing, it would backfire, and he would wind up having to put all of his energy into something that didn't help him or his client base.

I encouraged Camden to pursue more involvement in social media as long as those actions felt as if they were in alignment with him and with his vision. I told him that I viewed the business opportunity of social media as an extension of my true self, so I made using it into a spiritual practice, and I hoped that he would do the same. Putting energy into a community creates a greater positive feedback loop than putting energy into a solo venture. We talked about how I integrated social media into my life and my business practices and what I avoided. I focused on how I try to remain honest and true to myself even on my professional accounts. If I allow a separation between my business and personal accounts on an internal level, I find it much harder to keep the balance. If instead I allow my personal and professional values to integrate across my social media accounts, I'm better at maintaining the balance necessary for integrity.

Social media, when used both personally and professionally, allows for such a great public expression of positivity and energy. Camden had seen a lot of professional accounts that only focused on the business aspects of what social media can help you gain, without seeing what it can help create within a community—or even how it can help *form* a community. Running social media for your business doesn't have to—and shouldn't—feel like work. It should be a connection with your audience, with your community, that you wouldn't otherwise have. Social media isn't a narcissistic practice unless you make it one. It's community building and networking for both business and friendship.

By using our professional accounts to also discuss ideas and concepts that matter to us personally, we open ourselves up to greater opportunities for raising awareness about our businesses or about something we are deeply passionate about, such as a cause, charity, or fundraising event. I look to social media as a way to ask how I can be kind, loving, positive, and of service to my community.

It took a while for Camden to see these possibilities, but once he did, he welcomed the opportunities it provided with open arms. He changed his perspective on what social media really can do and allowed its positive energies into his life. As a result, he has attracted greater interest in his business and has developed an engaged social network community, both of which have had a positive impact on the success of his business.

I see social media as an extension of us as people, as human beings. It allows us to connect with people we might have otherwise never met. This generates a huge, positive network of like-minded people who are capable of creating great change. Similar to the way mantras work—where the energy you tap into has been built upon by thousands or millions of people—social media has access to a wealth of energy and the possibility of creating intense, meaningful relationships across the globe.

My follower base on Twitter, Facebook, and other platforms built themselves because I didn't see it as work. I saw it as a way to connect and share with other people.

Creating Balance

Creating balance in your life is an important investment in your future growth and prosperity. When one area of your life demands the bulk of your time, an imbalance is created in that area, and you will inevitably feel that imbalance in other areas of your life.

There are three keys to creating balance:

1. **Do what you love.** Work should be fun! It shouldn't feel like work, and it shouldn't feel separate from your personal life. Your work and personal lives should be entwined, to a healthy extent. You should be able to go out and have fun with friends and family, but you should also be having fun at work and feel a sense of enjoyment while working.

2. **Cultivate a spiritual practice.** This can include things such as meditation or taking a walk in Nature. This practice should help you find your center and give your mind a break from thinking about your To-Do List, so that you're better able to focus on your spiritual development. Without spiritual development, we cut ourselves off from a huge portion of the energy that the Universe is willing to give us.

3. **Play.** This one always makes my clients grin. Play can come in many forms, from things like drawing, painting, or playing an instrument, to literal playing—running around the yard with your kids or going to an amusement park. It's your time to turn off your mind and to just let loose. You might prefer play when it's in the form of

going to the movies or putting together a dinner party with your friends. Either way, play is crucial for all stages of life and development.

These three keys allow for balance in your life between work and personal time. It's important to keep your own energy "cup" full, so you can both give to and receive from others. If your cup is perpetually full, you might want to find time to give a bit more. If your cup is always running dry, remember to let others give to you, and to honor them by accepting their gifts.

Your cup running dry might also be a symptom of being out of alignment, so make sure to double-check that what you're doing in each area of your life is making you happy.

PROSPERITY PROCESSES:

INVESTING IN YOURSELF

These prosperity processes will help you to invest in yourself, not only by allowing you to take time for yourself, every day, but also by helping you to refocus your energies on what you really want and hope to achieve.

Personal Time

Everyone needs a little bit of time to themselves every day. We also have days when we need a little bit more personal time than others. Taking time for ourselves allows us to relax, regroup, and prepare for the next stretch of our journey.

STEP 1: Settle in somewhere comfortable with a pen and paper, in a quiet place where you can take 5 or 10 minutes to yourself.

STEP 2: Ask yourself, "What can I do to relax more?"

STEP 3: Write down 10 ideas. These ideas might be for things that take 5 minutes to do or an hour.

STEP 4: Carve out a small chunk of time every day this week, then devote that time in your mind to enjoying one of the relaxing practices you listed. Schedule this time as seriously as you would a doctor's appointment, and commit to it.

STEP 5: Actually do one of the things on your list—maybe you'll paint your nails, read a book, or go for a massage. The important thing is that this is a moment in time for you and no one else.

Investing in you and creating personal time for yourself will go a long way toward making you feel more relaxed and at peace with yourself and your surroundings.

Anchoring Balance

Creating and maintaining balance in our busy lives can be challenging. This process can help you rebalance your life:

STEP 1: Find a quiet place where you can have a little bit of time for yourself. Bring a piece of paper and a pen.

STEP 2: Reflect on your work and personal life. Write down how and where they intersect.

STEP 3: Take a moment of silence to focus on the connections between your work and personal life. Breathing deeply, imagine the two sections of your life intertwining, then blending into each other and becoming inseparable.

STEP 4: Think of a way to bring your work life and your personal life together in a respectful way—maybe you could host a weekend picnic for your coworkers and encourage them to bring their families with them.

These steps allow us to see how our work and personal lives are just two parts of our greater whole. In order to have balance, we need to ensure that our needs are being met in each part of our lives.

Making Time to Play

Most people spend their days giving to others. This can make it especially challenging to set time aside just for play. But it's crucial to give yourself playtime to recharge your energies and refresh your outlook. That energy helps you create and maintain all kinds of prosperity in your life, both inner and outer.

This process can help:

STEP 1: Find a quiet place where you can have a little bit of time for yourself. Bring a piece of paper and a pen.

STEP 2: Think about activities that made you happy when you were younger, whether they were creative, constructive, silly, or just fun. Write them down.

STEP 3: Flip the sheet of paper over and write down as many ways as you can come up with for how you can play now, whether it's literal childlike play, hosting a party, going dancing, playing a game, or going to the movies.

STEP 4: Create a place in your weekly schedule at least twice a week to spend an hour or more just for play. This is an appointment you have with yourself. Honor this commitment. It's as important as your commitment to daily chanting or meditating, eating well, or working.

Building Your Business

Investing in yourself is also about investing in your dreams and desires, especially when they are work related.

This might involve taking a class at your local college, reading a book, or participating in a seminar. There is no wrong way to build your business or professional role, as long as you feel that you are staying in alignment with your goals.

STEP 1: Make time every week to have a sit-down with yourself for a good brainstorming session.

STEP 2: Write down three or more ways that you would like to expand your business.

STEP 3: For each larger goal, write down the small, short-term steps you'll need to take to achieve each of those new directions. Work toward implementing one of those ways every week.

You don't need to fully implement a new expansion each week. Start by taking small, steady steps to get there. These expansions don't have to take a lot of time or money, especially if you don't have the cash flow yet. It can be as simple as attending a mixer and making new business contacts.

Once you do have cash flow available to expand your business or professional skills, I invite you to use it to literally invest in yourself, whether that means taking a class in business accounting, attending a conference in your field to make new contacts and expand your outlook, or reading a book on marketing. Putting time and money into your work wisely will only generate further prosperity and expansion.

Discipline, Organization, and Consistency

When I first began actively pursuing prosperity, one of the more challenging things that I had to learn was how to be disciplined, organized, and consistent in my actions. These three habits not only show a high professional ethic. They also present you as someone who is dependable and respectful of others—someone with a high standard, whom others will want to work with.

There are clear ways to do this and form great habits at the same time:

Be on time. It's always disrespectful to be late. Whether you're on your way to attend a mastermind group or to a coffee meeting with a prospective client, being on time is crucial. People tend to trust and want to help others whom they feel respect them, and one way we show respect to one another is by arriving promptly at the agreed-upon time.

When we are late—especially if we don't call or text ahead of time to explain the delay—we're showing a lack of consideration for other people. We are saying that our time is more important than theirs, which simply isn't true. We need to honor their time as much as we value our own. By doing this, we create a pattern of mutual respect and affirmation.

Show up organized. By being organized and showing up to the meeting with all the information and materials we need, we are giving the impression that we are responsible and capable. If we show up without some of our work tools, paperwork, or business cards, we're giving everyone present the idea that we don't care. This can create a challenging atmosphere of low vibrational energy. We want to encourage an open, affirming, high vibrational atmosphere that is conducive to prosperity and growth.

Free yourself of clutter. A simple way to assist you to become more organized is to simplify, or declutter, your life. The energy of clutter takes up space and can prevent us from moving forward, or it can just slow us down in achieving our goals (for example, clutter might make you late for appointments because you can't locate certain documents). Clutter can take the form of many different things and is not just physical; it can also be mental, emotional, spiritual, and financial. When we declutter or simplify, we create more space to attract the things we desire into our life. Think about the last time you had a big clean-out of your home or work space—I can almost guarantee that you felt better and lighter.

In addition to creating more space, decluttering also opens up the opportunity to give in service to the community and promotes the energy of circulation. Clothing, furniture, and items that are in good condition but no longer used can be donated to charities or shelters to aid those in need.

The accumulation of clutter is somewhat insidious, seemingly creeping up on us before we realize it's gotten out of hand. So it pays to be mindful in how we manage it in order to maintain a healthy balance. As you simplify your life, you will notice an improved flow and fluidity in your day-to-day dealings, as your energy is focused only on what serves your greatest good.

When I was just starting out in counseling, I worked

with Rosalie for a while. Rosalie was so positive and uplifting, every moment with her was a complete joy. She was a mom, an entrepreneur, and a coach. She was juggling so much that it continually amazed me how full of energy and positivity she was. She said it was just her nature and she was always that way. But while it attracted clients to her, she had a very difficult time keeping them. There were always new clients waiting, but older clients seemed to lose patience with her after a while. It didn't take me long to figure out why.

When she was late for our first appointment, it didn't surprise me. We were meeting at a halfway point between our offices, and neither of us was familiar with the area or the parking. But, after the second meeting it became clear that Rosalie had a bit of a problem with being on time and being organized. I had given her some homework after our previous meeting—I wanted her to list out her responsibilities and write down who helped her achieve everything that she does. I wanted to know more about her support network and how they helped her (something we talk more about in another chapter). When she showed up to our meeting, she was late and had left her list on her kitchen table that morning before she left for work.

I jumped at that opportunity to work with her on her organization. Together, Rosalie and I focused on organizing her calendar, using a few common tricks to make sure that she got where she needed to be on time, such as leaving a buffer zone around appointments so she wouldn't be late and setting her phone and car clocks a little fast.

She found that by being punctual and keeping her files and appointments organized, she had a huge increase in repeat clients and a dramatic jump in her Yelp rating. People had never complained about the services she provided, only that she wasn't very professional in how she performed them. She hasn't received an "unprofessional" comment since making these changes.

By pursuing discipline, organization, and consistency, we open ourselves up to many opportunities that may have otherwise passed us by. Walking the balance between fluidity and discipline is the key. We can be free-spirited and open while still being focused, organized, and consistent.

Simplify and Declutter Your Life

There are many ways to simplify and clear away the clutter we have accumulated in our lives. Clearing the clutter in our homes or work space can be easily achieved with a minimal amount of time and effort. Physical clutter is the easiest to address, because it is tangible and always visible. The other forms of clutter may not be so obvious.

One form of clutter happens when we become so busy we feel overwhelmed. An easy way to simplify your life is by looking at your lifestyle and determining if your activities are a true desire, a need, or have become a habit that no longer serves any real purpose and therefore is just becoming clutter.

Here are a few easy steps that can help to alleviate the energy of clutter around you and allow more space for what truly makes your heart sing to come in. This exercise is an extension of your Joy List that you created in Foundation #1. You will need some paper and a pen or pencil for this exercise.

STEP 1: Find yourself a comfortable place where you will not be disturbed.

STEP 2: Take a few moments to reflect on your life and write down your current lifestyle activities, hobbies, sports, or other commitments. You may also want to include activities such as dining out.

STEP 3: Now reflect on each activity. Why did you start it in the first place? How do you feel when you attend this activity? Are you still interested in the activity? What purpose does it serve? What would your life look like if you no longer attended this activity?

STEP 4: Reflect on the items on your Joy List and ask yourself if there is anything on that list you would prefer to do instead of the items on your Current Activities list.

STEP 5: Decide which activities you want to let go of now. Gratefully release these activities from your life, thanking them for all that they have afforded you, and make the switch.

It is important to note that this exercise is not about replacing one form of clutter with another. If something is no longer serving us in any way, it will deplete our energy. Replacing it with something that brings us joy and is in alignment with our purpose brings us happiness, and as we now know, happiness results in prosperity.

This is a good exercise to repeat several times a year, especially if you are finding yourself feeling drained of energy and constantly busy.

Decluttering Your Surroundings

Because physical clutter is easily visible, it can be easier to address than internal clutter. Wardrobes, cupboards, and drawers often contain so many items that we can quickly identify as things we no longer like or need.

It's important to deal with physical clutter. It can drain your energy as a constant reminder of half-finished chores and unfulfilled plans. This keeps you from feeling in control of your environment and from relaxing in your home or work space when you have free time.

Clutter is also an eyesore. We need beauty, order, and open space in our surroundings. A lack of these can bring our energy down and even affect our self-esteem.

Here are a few easy steps to help alleviate physical clutter—this applies to your desk drawers but works for any space at home or at work:

STEP 1: Pull every single item out of your desk drawers so they're completely empty.

STEP 2: Make four piles: Give Away, Keep, Throw Away, and Recycle.

STEP 3: Put everything still usable but no longer needed by you (such as too many pens, pads of paper, and paper clips) in a bag, ready to go to a charity thrift shop or to someone else who can use them.

STEP 4: Create an organized space for the items you need to keep. If they are important documents, such as tax forms, a deed, or a lease, put them in a file folder that is clearly labeled. Organize the remaining items in the drawers into a logical order, so that you can find things quickly when you need them.

STEP 5: Recycle the remaining items, throwing away only the things you can't recycle.

STEP 6: Repeat this process with cupboards, dresser drawers, and closets at home. Be ruthless! If you haven't used something in the past year and it has no real meaning for you or anyone in your family, let it go.

STAYING ORGANIZED AND ON TIME

Most successful people—people who live healthy, fulfilling lives, and who handle their money and responsibilities with confidence—have methods and habits in place that help them stay organized. Being organized and on time helps us feel positive and energetic. That emotional state not only feels great, it also helps to increase the flow of abundance in our lives. And it helps keep every part of our lives in alignment with our bigger vision.

A big part of your prosperity is feeling great about your day! You want to feel cared for and in the flow of all the good that the Universe has for you. To stay in alignment with that flow, we need not only people but also methods and habits that support us. To arrive on time, for example, many people use a method like the one Rosalie and I used—set your clocks 15 minutes ahead, or set

(continued)

alarms on your smartphone: one that tells you when to get ready for an appointment and one that tells you when it's time to leave.

Another great way to stay in control of your day: write a daily schedule. Give everything important in your day—meditation, work, play, cooking a healthy dinner, et cetera—its own time slot, so that no important activity gets accidentally left behind.

Methods like these don't only help you get your work done and remember to pick up the kids—they also help you take better care of yourself. See these methods as friends who quietly support you, saving you from extra work, worry, and the empty-cup feeling that comes from being disorganized.

You deserve to feel joyful and fulfilled every day—making time for everything that's important to you, while still being kind to yourself. Being organized and on time can help you get there.

Summary

Investing in yourself is about much more than getting the skills, training, and the right work clothes to do well out in the world. Those things are fine, but they are not enough. You need to give to yourself as much as you give to the world.

No matter what is happening in your life, you need time to rest and play. You deserve time away from work and chores, and time out in Nature. You also deserve to do the kind of work that you really enjoy and to have a work life that is aligned with your personal values. You deserve to be your true self at work, as well as at home.

Investing in yourself also means investing in your work in ways that will reap benefits for you now and in the future. That might mean reading a great how-to, getting some counseling, taking a class in an area that interests you, or decluttering your home or work space—whatever expands your life in ways that are aligned with your true self.

Being disciplined, organized, and on time will help others know they can trust you to be reliable and have a high professional standard. It will also help ensure that every important part of your life has a definite place in your schedule.

All of these ideas will help you lift your energy higher. They'll help you value and protect your time and your energy. And they'll keep you energized and organized, so that you're ready and able to welcome greater levels of prosperity into your life.

Building a Support Network

Itakes a village to prosper. As Jack Canfield, creator of the *Chicken Soup for the Soul* series, has said, "Success in life is not possible without building and nurturing strong relationships."

These include your relationships to other people, your job or business, and yourself. You can generate an atmosphere of prosperity on your own, but collaborating with others and keeping yourself accountable to them will make fostering that prosperity easier.

Building and aligning with people, places, and situations that support you will help you transition more easily into your new, more prosperous journey. When Leslie approached me after a talk I gave, she told me that she was just starting a business in a new city and she was worried that it would immediately fail because she didn't have many local contacts. Her business was both online and brick-and-mortar, but she was worried that without a lot of local buzz, she wouldn't be able to keep either side of it running. I was in town for another week, so we made time for coffee a couple of days later.

Over coffee, we talked about how important the idea of "the village" is. Most of the time, when you hear people talking about "it takes a village," they are generally talking about raising kids. It takes a lot more than just the parents to make sure that the kids are happy, healthy, and well adjusted. Think of your business as a child who needs to be nurtured.

Businesses don't survive well alone. They need support— the business equivalent of neighborhood kids, grandparents, and birthday celebrations—in order to thrive. They can survive in a vacuum, but it doesn't mean that they're going to prosper or be happy. By finding your network—your village— you can help your business survive. I encouraged Leslie to go to a couple of local meetups and networking events to meet people in the area. Even if you don't meet anyone in your field, that doesn't mean that they don't know people who could use your services. Word of mouth is powerful. Leslie disclosed that she had plans to go to an event that weekend, but she also wanted to build her online profile and wasn't sure how to do so without blatantly pushing her product. I told her that the village she was seeking wasn't about her product or even her business. It was about her.

If she could find people who would encourage her, talk about her, and support her, then she and her business would flourish. I expressed to her that if she engaged with a community and gave to them by putting positive energy out, she would receive it back. The Universe doesn't take more than you can give and it never gives more than you can take. The most important thing that I conveyed to Leslie was to *not* focus on getting new clients but rather on making new friends.

Building a village isn't about expanding your client base; it's about supporting one another. The village might never directly bring you a new client, but if your support network is strong and healthy, it will help you keep the clients you do attract and will help keep you in alignment with your goals and your vision. By building or joining a community, whether online or in person, you immediately open yourself up to bigger and greater things.

I recently received an e-mail from Leslie updating me on her progress. Her business had taken off after a couple of months of making new contacts, creating social media profiles, and joining several online and offline communities for hobbies and other interests she has. One of her best clients was brought to her not by a business associate or through networking but by one of the women that she talks to online over their shared love of corgis.

People who are pessimistic don't contribute to the high vibrational energy necessary for a prosperous atmosphere and energy. If we instead surround ourselves with people who promote positivity and who are actively pursuing their own prosperity, their energy—coupled with our own—will work together and multiply.

Even if your support network is just one or two people at first, that's great! Keep in mind that we all start out on this journey alone and that it can take a while before we pull other people into our orbit. We have to see ourselves as our own support network first, so that it can start expanding.

A support system can start with just a couple of people you meet on Twitter or Facebook or through a Meetup group. The important thing is that you are getting out there and making connections.

The more you do this, the more word will spread, and the bigger your village will become.

Mastermind Group

A mastermind group is a group of people who brainstorm, or as I like to say, heartstorm together, and hold one another accountable for meeting personally set deadlines and goals.

Mastermind groups offer accountability, education, and support. They can become your village and help you to achieve the prosperity and success goals you've set for yourself.

The members of a mastermind group have chosen to be there. It isn't a class or a coaching session. It's a place where people get together to talk about what they have achieved, what they want to achieve in the future, and how to meet those goals. These groups are usually confidential, and the people involved are committed to helping one another. Members are catalysts for one another's growth and successes. Though you can network within a mastermind group, that is not its purpose. Its purpose is to foster mutual support and accountability while the members of the group pursue their dreams.

You can start a mastermind group by asking friends if they or anyone they know is interested in joining one. You can also start a Meetup group or, if you use social media—which I highly recommend—you can start an online mastermind group with your Twitter followers or Facebook friends.

Being held accountable for your actions and pursuits is an incredibly helpful motivator, especially for those of us who may have a hard time hunkering down and getting started on those first few steps toward our vision!

PROSPERITY PROCESSES:

BUILDING A SUPPORT SYSTEM

These prosperity processes will help you to strengthen your own self-support while creating a comprehensive support network around yourself.

The network might be online, in person, or both, so don't be shy about trying any or all of these ideas. The goal is to have a group that you can be held accountable to for your work and that provides positive, high vibrational energy in your life.

Mastermind Group

Working together toward prosperity is a great way to foster your own growth and be of service to others. You can achieve this with a mastermind group.

Depending on where you live, you may be able to find a mastermind group in your area through Craigslist, Meetup, or Facebook. If you would rather create your own group, all you need are two or more people coming together to hold each other accountable for taking action on their long- and short-range goals.

Mastermind groups thrive on the power of members being accountable to and supportive of one another. The group can be online, in-person within your community, or a combination of those, as long as the group meets consistently. Generally, I've found that mastermind groups that meet at least once a month are the most successful at helping members reach their goals.

If you choose to start your own group, here are a few steps for running a meeting:

STEP 1: First, ask everyone to share their positives for that month. For example, "I reached out to a dozen potential new clients and had meetings with five of them."

STEP 2: Have everyone share their new goal, stating what they would like the others to hold them accountable for at the next meeting.

STEP 3: Close the meeting with shared gratitudes. Start with the phrase "I am so grateful for . . ."

Social Networking

Social media, especially when you're first starting out, can be a bit daunting! There are so many different apps and websites to choose from, that it can feel overwhelming.

Before leaping into this process, I highly recommend that you sit down and research what platform you want to go with first. This doesn't have to be your only foray into social media, but it can be if that's the one that works best for you.

STEP 1: Make your chosen platform an extension of yourself. Personalize your avatar and profile. Make sure the things you post are a clear representation of what you want to present to the world.

STEP 2: Every day, set the intention to share in a positive way. You might ask yourself something like, "What can I share today that can really help bring people together?"

STEP 3: Reach out to other like-minded people and connect with them. This can help you to bring people together, so that you can all create a community and a support network.

STEP 4: Share others' social media posts. This helps foster new relationships and create a sense of community.

By using social media as an extension of yourself and your practices, you'll be better able to stick with your new habits well past those first 28 days. Connecting positively with people around the world is an enlightening experience, and I highly recommend it to everyone.

Host a Social Mixer

Beyond Meetups and social networking, you can also reach out within your own social circle to meet new people. In addition to making new friends, you might also find that some of them are able to help you stay on track with your goals. Together, you can build a network of support for one another.

STEP 1: Invite six or eight people to an evening out, whether you know them from social media or face-to-face, and encourage them to bring a friend. You might want to meet up at a bar or restaurant the first few times.

STEP 2: Set a theme for the gathering. This could be just for fun (such as a "Wear a Strange Hat" party) or it could be work-related (such as a "Come Dressed as the Person You Really Want to Be" or a "Bring a List of Your Biggest Dreams" meetup). Set whatever theme you feel will best help people connect. As you and your group come to know one another, you can narrow it down a bit. If possible, invite not only personal friends, but work friends as well. You never know whom you'll meet! This gathering might even develop into a mastermind group!

STEP 3: Make sure you talk to everyone you've invited, even if it's just for a minute or two. You never know what the person in the corner has to say or knows about but is too shy to say without encouragement.

Getting together with friends and friends of friends is one of the best ways to expand both your social circle and your support network.

Summary

It really does take a village.

We can't do everything by ourselves, and we aren't as alone as we might think we are. Everyone can develop the opportunities to meet more people, as well as build up the relationships they already have.

The purpose of this foundation is to help you ready yourself and generate a support network so that you can better develop your life path. Investing in our dreams and ourselves is just as important as discovering our dreams to begin with.

Practicing Gratitude and Kindness

Gratitude is an immensely powerful form of emotion, thought, and energy.

When we're thankful, both verbally and emotionally, we give ourselves permission to feel good about our lives. We allow ourselves to be content, in the moment, with what we already have. This generates an environment of high vibrational energy and attraction by promoting happiness, joy, and prosperity. That high vibrational energy pulls other helpful forces to it, creating a positive feedback loop.

That feedback loop forges enthusiasm, determination, and focus. When we're feeling good, when we're feeling thankful and grateful, we attract stronger bonds between ourselves, our families and friends, and our work. This lowers stress levels and enables more interpersonal warmth in our interactions with others.

Gratitude has the power to promote and create comfort and peace within us. When we are thankful for even the smallest things in life, we are more aware of the powerful energy and forces around us that are constantly trying to help us. Gratitude opens doors within us and creates opportunities for growth where few, if any, existed before.

I've never met a client that came to me feeling as hopeless as Mario did. Mario was battling depression—his business had folded in the 2009 economic crash and after struggling to find work, he'd been repeatedly laid off. His depression was coupled with a deep sense of failure. Whenever Mario entered into a new job, he did so enthusiastically. He wanted to make it work even if he didn't love the job. He wanted to make his family proud. He was never let go for doing a poor job, but he was nevertheless laid off again and again as businesses struggled. His bosses were always sad to see him go, but their hands were tied.

Mario's resulting depression made it difficult for him to see what he did have, instead of only what he thought he was lacking. We worked together using gratitude processes to help him internalize how much he did have to be thankful for. This helped him not only to seek help for his depression, but also to feel worthy of doing so. He no longer felt he was a burden to his family.

Mario began to focus on how grateful he was to have the support of his family throughout his battle with depression and multiple layoffs. He was grateful for how well his children were doing in school, for how strong his wife was for shouldering the financial burden, and for how brave his brother's family was as they dealt with their own setbacks and challenges. He found his gratitude and made sure to remind himself daily of what he *did* have. The repetition and routine helped him out of his depression and back into his family's life.

After deciding that part of the problem was how unhappy he was working for someone else, Mario began to rebuild his company. His family struggled to live on one income but found they could make it work while he restarted his business. Then the economy took an upturn in his area, and his business took off. When I checked in with Mario several months later, he was still doing the gratitude processes and focusing on what he had, instead of what he thought he needed. In thinking that he desperately needed a job to support his family, he went after opportunities that weren't right for him or the company he was hired into. Once Mario let go of this misconception, he was better able to rebuild his business and focus on doing what made him happy.

In the hustle and bustle of modern life, it's not unusual to forget about what we do want, while we're so relentlessly pursuing what we don't want, out of a sense of obligation to something or someone else. Making time every day to count our blessings is hugely beneficial for promoting prosperity in our daily lives. Remember that prosperity isn't just monetary; it's also the happiness and fulfillment you find in your life.

How can you be happy with your life if you're not grateful for what you already have?

Kindness Fundamentals

In the midst of our busy schedules, it's important—not only for ourselves but for the sake of others—to take the time to be kind.

As we rush through our daily lives, we often forget to thank the people who make them possible. Without the cashier at the store, you would have a much more difficult time getting your groceries. Without your coworkers, you would have a much more difficult time doing your job. Without the baristas of the world, we would all be significantly less caffeinated. Simple acts of kindness might take the form of leaving your barista your change as a tip or smiling at the checkout lady and thanking her for bagging your groceries.

Smiling and saying "Thank you!" are two huge ways to express both kindness and gratitude to the people around us. Everyone has a few seconds to stop and be kind and grateful. Taking a moment to do this enriches our lives and energy, while promoting good will and positivity all around us. When we show kindness, we show that we care. Being kind and pleasant generates high vibrational energy around us and invites in happiness and prosperity.

I have a close friend, Henry, who once owned a small, independent holistic pharmacy. He would tell me the most hilarious, horrendous, and heartbreaking stories about his customers. He once told me that even though 70 percent of his customers were polite, and 25 percent were kind, it was always the 4 percent who were rude that he remembered.

I then asked him about the remaining 1 percent of his customers. He smiled for a moment and looked me in the eye.

"That last 1 percent," he said, "make my day. Those are the people who ask how my day is going, or who smile and say 'Thank you.' They go out of their way to make sure that our transaction is pleasant. They're my favorite customers, and they are why I do what I do."

That message stuck with me, and when I met Rachel, I understood why the Universe thought it was so important that I receive that message. Kindness is about the little interactions throughout our day, but it is also good business. Rachel rushed through her life like a tornado across the plains. She ran a non-profit afterschool program that focused on helping at-risk kids. Rachel had experienced decent success promoting the program with families, but she was having a very difficult time getting businesses to participate.

She came to me to try to figure out how to entice and encourage more businesses to get involved with her program. She didn't want to have to close the program, but without a certain number of participants, she would lose her funding. She had tried everything she could think of and was starting to feel worn out and that her work was unappreciated.

After hearing about how she "sold" her program to businesses, I suggested that she try a slightly new tactic: slowing down. Her responsibilities were limitless, and she ran the program almost singlehandedly, so when she went to ask a business owner for their support, she tended to quickly overload them with information. She took a numbers approach to the situation: the more you ask, the greater chance you have of someone saying yes. I asked that for a week, she only approach one company. For that week, she should slowly encourage and ask for that potential client's support.

Because she was taking her time, she was better able to assess what the company needed from her. By tackling only one company that week, she was able to relax and take a deep breath, which did wonders for her overall attitude and energy levels. Since she was better able to keep her own energy cup full, she felt more able to give to the potential client she approached. Rachel could smile and enjoy the conversation, because talking with them was her only appointment for the day. She had the time to engage them in conversation and have an exchange of energy and ideas, rather than forcing herself and her program at them.

Rachel became the 1 percent customer instead of the 70 percent. She became memorable instead of forgettable, and soon became invested in the company she was trying to recruit. It was the little things that endeared the potential client to her and her cause. She asked how the managers were doing. She smiled when she said hello and was interested in what they had to say. She took time to listen to their concerns and to address them, instead of writing them off. Rachel came to know the managers, the staff, and the owner. The company heads said yes to her program and brought another three companies along. Her kindness and gratitude attracted more business in one week than her straightforward facts and statistics approach had in a month.

She not only helped the kids in her program and the businesses she recruited, but also encouraged the staff and families to participate, allowing her to expand the program and help even more at-risk kids.

Kindness and gratitude go a long way toward helping those around us to also have a pleasant and prosperous life. Without Rachel's foray into a kinder, gentler approach, her program would have floundered, and the kids she was trying to help wouldn't have been able to get the services they needed.

PROSPERITY PROCESSES:

GRATITUDE

The following gratitude and kindness processes will help to anchor the foundation of gratitude in your life.

Doing these will help you focus more clearly on the things you have now, rather than the things you want. It can be a struggle to stay in the now and be thankful during our busy, everyday lives. These processes seek to eliminate that struggle and make gratitude and kindness fun and easy breezy.

Saying Your Morning Gratitudes

Like most people, I have a morning ritual that I go through every day when I wake up: I get up, shower, brush my teeth, make some breakfast, and check my e-mail. I also say my morning gratitudes.

But before I even get out of bed, I think of five things—big or small—that I'm grateful for. I encourage you to add this daily practice to your life.

Depending on your current situation, it may be more challenging to do this some days than others. I've definitely had days where I struggled to come up with five things because I was too caught up in my own mind to see what I had. If you find yourself thinking along those same lines, focus on what's immediately at hand: your warm bed, your alarm clock that went off on time, the sun or rain outside. Save the bigger, more complex topics for days when you can handle them.

Morning gratitudes aren't about coming up with all new

items every single morning or finding the best possible things to be thankful for. They're about appreciating everything in your life, no matter how big or small. By beginning your day in a state of gratitude, you immediately foster an environment of more gratitude and even more prosperity.

It starts your day off right and opens doors for more high vibrational energy and growth to occur. The more we have to be grateful for, the more positive energy we carry, which encourages even more growth.

The Gratitude Game

This is an ongoing practice—I encourage you to keep it in your mind and expand upon it throughout your day.

STEP 1: Get a pen and paper or a little notepad. Write down all the things you are grateful for.

STEP 2: Periodically throughout the day, jot down new items as you think of them.

STEP 3: Share your list with someone. This can be done in person, through e-mail, over the phone, or via social media.

This exercise encourages you to be grateful for both the big and little things in your life. Keeping in mind all of the things you are thankful for as you go through the day promotes not only prosperity, but also happiness and joy. It encourages you to think of positive, motivational things in your life that are helping you both personally and professionally.

Sharing your gratitudes creates the energy of multiplying abundance and growth. It also encourages others to feel grateful for what they have and to play the game of gratitude for themselves.

The Gratitude Dance

This is one of my favorite processes! I love to dance. It makes me feel free and loved, and best of all, it's fun!

This process works together with the Gratitude Game, so make sure you've started with that one first.

STEP 1: If you can, change into some comfortable clothes that you can move in easily.

STEP 2: Gather together your list of gratitudes from the Gratitude Game and a radio, MP3 player, YouTube connection, or cell phone—anything that has a happy, upbeat song on it that you love.

STEP 3: Hold your gratitudes over your heart area, right below your collarbone. Take a moment to set the intention of giving gratitude to the Universe for what you have.

STEP 4: Turn on your song and dance! While dancing, say or sing all the items on your list!

STEP 5: When the song ends, take another moment to quietly thank the Universe for everything that you have.

This process uses physical movement and energy to help you open up to the energy of positive thinking all around you.

If you want to go on a little longer and do two or three songs, that's great! Remember to set a clear intention and recite your gratitudes each time.

The Importance of Smiling

Did you know that smiling releases "feel good" chemicals in the brain that activate a sense of well-being and joy?[1]

Throughout the world, a smile can get you much more than a frown. Receiving a smile from anyone always brightens our day. It has been scientifically proven that both smiling and seeing smiling faces actually makes us happier.

I invite you to smile as much as possible every day. This promotes happiness within us and happiness within the Universe as a whole.

Every time you purchase something, smile at the cashier.

Every time you say hi to someone, do it with a smile.

Every time you walk into a store, smile at the greeter.

The more you smile, the more natural it will feel and the happier you will be. This process creates a positive feedback loop within your life that stretches beyond just your immediate social circle.

You never know whose day you can make better just by offering them a simple smile.

---

1 Sarah Stevenson, "There's Magic in Your Smile," PsychologyToday.com, (June 25, 2012) psychologytoday.com/blog/cutting-edge-leadership /201206/there-s-magic-in-your-smile.

Summary

Gratitude and kindness do not exist in limited quantities.

We all have the capacity for limitless expression of these feelings. By embracing the processes and ideas put forth in this foundation of expressing gratitude, you open yourself up to making the world a happier, more thankful place, while making yourself a happier, more thankful person.

This generates a huge force of positive energy in your life that can only bring you more prosperity.

Your 28-Day Easy Breezy Prosperity Plan

P lease use this plan however is best for you: feel free to add to the program or to tailor it until it feels the most joyous to you. The purpose of this 28-Day Prosperity Plan is simply to get the ball rolling toward the manifestation of your own desired reality. Have fun with it, and be gentle with yourself throughout the whole process. One of my intentions in developing this plan is to give you the option of completing the processes at your own pace. You may decide to complete only one or two processes each day, if and when they are convenient, or you may wish to commit to the more intense, fuller version of the plan. It is totally up to you. This plan is only meant to serve as a guide. If there are processes that you have already fully integrated into your lifestyle, then that's great. It means that you are on your way to achieving more prosperity in your life.

As with all new things, we are more likely to achieve greater results if we honor our bodies and ourselves by being in the healthiest condition we can be. By establishing and engaging in healthy sleep and rest patterns, exercise routines, and a healthy diet, we are providing a solid foundation to build on, whether it be physically, mentally, emotionally, or spiritually. Subsequently, an integral part of this 28-day plan is to be conscious of the above so that we are open to receive all the blessings the Universe has to offer.

As you commit to this plan, I ask that through the course of this cycle you set your alarm to go off half an hour earlier than you would normally get up, so that what you are about to embark on isn't started off in a rush. Don't worry; I also want you to go to bed half an hour earlier, so you are not missing out on needed rest!

Having a shower in the morning will get you into the right space to begin your day, as it not only invigorates and "awakens" all your senses, it also strengthens your immune system and instantly raises your state of well-being, which is a great start to the day. In addition, make the conscious decision to eat healthy foods at each meal that are jam-packed with natural vitamins, minerals, and nutrients that energize the body and help it to thrive. These foods include natural and organic living foods, such as fresh veggies, nuts, seeds, fruits, and light proteins. Limit your sugar and starchy carbohydrate intake, so that you have more sustained energy throughout the day.

The plan incorporates all the processes covered in the book. Some are meant to be done daily, others throughout the week, and some as a one-off throughout the first 28 days. The first nine processes are to be completed daily; you will need to refer back to them each day until you become familiar with them. Some processes only take five minutes, while others take longer. But there is no hard and fast rule on length of time, and I encourage you to do what feels comfortable for you. The intention is that these processes will be easily incorporated into your life and become a normal way of being.

Before you commence Day 1 of the 28-Day Prosperity Plan, I would ask you to consider the following two questions: "What does 'prosperity' mean to me?" and "What does 'money' mean to me?" Sit for a moment and write down the first thoughts that come to you, regardless of what they are. You only need to spend a few minutes doing this, then place those notes in a safe place.

At the end of the 28 days we will use this reference point to look back and see how far you have actually progressed. I have no doubt you will be amazed to see how far you've come!

If you find that you would like to continue on with this or a similar plan far beyond the initial 28 days, go for it! You deserve all of the blessings the Universe has in store for you, and this 28-Day Easy Breezy Prosperity Plan will support you in opening yourself up to receiving it all!

What does "prosperity" mean to me?

What does "money" mean to me?

EVERYDAY DAILY PROSPERITY STEPS

STEP 1

I set my alarm to wake me up 30 minutes earlier than usual.

STEP 2

Before getting out of bed, I express out loud or write down at least five (5) things I am grateful for, and share why I am grateful for these things. For example: I am grateful for my bed because it keeps me feeling cozy and comfortable while I'm sleeping. **(Morning Gratitudes, on page 93)**

STEP 3

After brushing my teeth in the morning, I smile for 20 to 30 seconds while looking in the bathroom mirror. The more cheesy and silly the smile, the better I feel. This helps me generate "feel good" chemicals in my brain that activate a sense of well-being and joy. **(Smiling, on page 96)**

STEP 4

I dedicate 15 to 30 minutes to doing my prosperity mantras. If I am driving in the car to work or running errands, I can also revisit these mantras throughout the day to magnify their potency. The prosperity mantras I use are: **Om gum ganapataye namaha** (Om guhm guh-nuh-puh-tuh-yea nah-mah-hah) clears obstacles to a happy, healthy, prosperous life. **Om shreem maha l'akshmye namaha** (Om shr-eem mah-hah lahk-shmee-yay nah-mah-hah) attracts prosperity in all areas of life. **Om breez namaha** (Om brah-zee nah-mah-hah) attracts good fortune and abundance. **(Prosperity Mantras, on page 16)**

STEP 5

I take periodic breaks throughout the day to rest my mind. I do this by finding an opportunity to be out in Nature and focus on being fully present with my five senses.

STEP 6

I smile more, all throughout the day, at all those I encounter. **(Smiling, on page 96)**

STEP 7

Throughout the day, I find some time to play and have fun. The key is to think less and feel more. Some ways I like to play are to jump on a rebounder (mini trampoline), sing, paint, watch a funny movie, or dance around the house.

STEP 8

At night, I reflect on all the wonderful things that happened throughout the day. I then do the 5-Step Money-Relationship Healing Process. This allows me to experience a deeper relationship with the money in my life, and it prepares me for the future prosperity that will be entering my life soon. The 5-Step Money-Relationship Healing Process liberates me from any misconceptions I've had about money! **(5-Step Money-Relationship Healing Process, on page 46)**

STEP 9

I go to bed 30 minutes earlier than usual, so that my body can receive some extra time to rejuvenate itself and so that it will have time to operate at its most optimum level the next day.

DAY 1

STEPS 1–9
Refer to Daily Processes 1 through 9
STEP 10
Throughout the day, anytime I am dealing with giving or receiving money, I do the Quick 2-Step Money-Relationship Healing Process. Usually I do this process in the privacy of my car after I have made a purchase at the store. I hold the receipt of my purchase over my chest and repeat the following statement: "Feed the hungry, shelter the homeless, bless those you come in contact with, and return to me manyfold." Repeating this or a similar statement allows me to remember that when I allow money to circulate in and out of my life, I am actually in the flow and when I am in the flow, I open myself up to many more blessings the Universe has in store for me. I repeat the statement in the Quick 2-Step Money-Relationship Healing Process, until any angst I feel around spending money has disappeared. (**Quick 2-Step Money-Relationship Healing Process, on page 47**)
STEP 11
I find at least one opportunity to be of service today through my time, energy, gifts, abilities, or any other way I may be able to contribute to someone in need.
STEP 12
In the late afternoon or early evening, I connect with a few friends for our weekly Mastermind Group session. During this safe and supportive time together, we set powerful intentions of what we'd like to create more of in our lives. We share some action steps we each will personally be completing in order to make our desired manifestations a reality. We also hold one another accountable throughout the week to make sure we are following through on some of these action steps toward manifesting our goals. (**Mastermind Group, on page 83**)

DAY 1 *Journal*

Did you complete Daily Processes 1-9? How did each step impact your day?

_____

_____

_____

_____

_____

What other steps did you complete today? What felt the most comfortable and/or challenging?

_____

_____

_____

_____

What are your goals for tomorrow?

_____

_____

_____

_____

Day 2

STEPS 1–9
Refer to Daily Processes 1 through 9
STEP 10
I create my **Joy List** by reflecting on the things that have or do bring me joy in my life or make my heart sing. I write each thing down on my list. I implement one, if not more, of the items on this list in my daily life. For example: "I will set aside 30 minutes to enjoy reading a good book every day." **(Joy List, on page 15)**
STEP 11
I withdraw a sum of money that I feel slightly uncomfortable with and carry it with me at all times, until I feel comfortable with that amount. By carrying larger amounts of cash, I am learning and placing my trust in the Universe, that the Universe not only takes care of me, but also provides for me and keeps me safe when I have a lot of money. **(Carrying Cash, on page 48)**
STEP 12
During my day, I take time to reflect on my work life and my personal life, identify where they intersect, and write this down. I imagine them merging together and becoming inseparable, and I come up with different ways that I can play or have fun, while still respecting all the aspects of me that make me whole. **(Anchoring Balance, on page 66)**

DAY 2 *Journal*

Did you complete Daily Processes 1-9? How did each step impact your day?

_____

_____

_____

_____

_____

What other steps did you complete today? What felt the most comfortable and/or challenging?

_____

_____

_____

_____

_____

What are your goals for tomorrow?

_____

_____

_____

_____

DAY 3

| **STEPS 1-9** |
| Refer to Daily Processes 1 through 9 |
| **STEP 10** |
| I open myself up to facing a fear or going outside of my comfort zone today. This may be as simple as saying hello to someone I have always been too shy to approach, making a suggestion at my workplace, or singing at a karaoke venue. |
| **STEP 11** |
| Today I commit to repaying a debt and moving toward bringing my financial situation back into the alignment of healthy circulation. It doesn't have to be the full amount, and it really doesn't matter if it is only a few dollars, as the energy of the intent is the focus. |
| **STEP 12** |
| In the morning I take a few moments to write down all the things I am grateful for. I add to this list during the course of my day and share it with others either in person, via phone, e-mail, or social media. This exercise reminds me of how thankful I am for everything in my life, both big and small, and how prosperous I already am. **(Gratitude Game, on page 94)** |

DAY 3 *Journal*

Did you complete Daily Processes 1-9? How did each step impact your day?

_____

_____

_____

_____

_____

What other steps did you complete today? What felt the most comfortable and/or challenging?

_____

_____

_____

_____

_____

What are your goals for tomorrow?

_____

_____

_____

_____

_____

Day 4

STEPS 1–9

Refer to Daily Processes 1 through 9

STEP 10

I make time today to explore **Social Networking** and identify which brand I feel the most comfortable with—that is, Facebook, Twitter, Instagram. I open an account, if I'm not already a user, and explore so I become familiar with the setup. I share a positive thought with the intent of bringing people together, ever mindful that the way I present myself on social media is just another extension of who I am. **(Social Networking, on page 84)**

STEP 11

I honor myself by making a list of at least 10 things I could implement that will help me relax more, as I acknowledge how important **Personal Time** is to my well-being. The list may include a regular massage, manicure or pedicure, or reading a favorite magazine in the garden. I implement at least one item on my list today, whether it takes 5 minutes or an hour. During this time, I am committed to "me" time, and try to be as free from distractions as possible. **(Personal Time, on page 65)**

STEP 12

Today I place a few dollars in some envelopes and leave them at random places throughout the day (for example, the market, car windows, workplace, notice boards). On these **Gift Envelopes**, I write something like "Buy yourself a coffee!" and that is all. In doing this process I am giving back, knowing I will make someone's day and not expect anything in return. **(Gift Envelopes, on page 50)**

Day 4 *Journal*

Did you complete Daily Processes 1-9? How did each step impact your day?

_____

_____

_____

_____

_____

What other steps did you complete today? What felt the most comfortable and/or challenging?

_____

_____

_____

_____

What are your goals for tomorrow?

_____

_____

_____

_____

DAY 5

STEPS 1–9

Refer to Daily Processes 1 through 9

STEP 10

During the day, I sit and create my **Quality List** by contemplating the qualities I want to embody in my life (for example, stability, freedom, happiness, flexibility, etc.). Reflecting on the things I would like in my life, (such as a relationship, more money, or a vacation) I will identify what qualities these will bring me (that is, "What quality does _____ provide for me?"). For example: "My relationship will provide me with friendship, comfort, intimacy, and affection." I then identify where the qualities I have determined are already in existence and present in my life.
(Quality List, on page 20)

STEP 11

I focus on my **Breathing,** taking full and deep breaths as I move through my day. If I notice that I am taking small shallow breaths, I stop what I am doing and take a few moments to concentrate on breathing deeply. It reminds me that when I take deeper and fuller breaths, I am actually sending out a powerful signal to the Universe that I am open to fuller and more abundant experiences in my life. I am mindful to no longer take shallow little breaths that are usually a sign one is living in a more survival–based "barely-getting-by" kind of existence.

STEP 12

I am open to experiencing **Fluidity** with my thoughts and actions. During the course of my day, if I am met with circumstances that are unexpected or that trigger me in some way, I make the conscious effort to halt my immediate reaction. I surrender any feelings of the need to control the events occurring around me, trusting that I am fully supported by the Universe.

DAY 5 *Journal*

Did you complete Daily Processes 1-9? How did each step impact your day?

_____

_____

_____

_____

_____

What other steps did you complete today? What felt the most comfortable and/or challenging?

_____

_____

_____

_____

What are your goals for tomorrow?

_____

_____

_____

_____

Day 6

STEPS 1-9

Refer to Daily Processes 1 through 9

STEP 10

During the course of my day, I have a brainstorming session in regards to **Building My Business**. I identify three (3) possible ways that I can expand upon my business, jotting down small steps to achieve this outcome. **(Building Your Business, on page 68)**

STEP 11

I am open to flexing my **Receiving** muscles today by allowing myself to receive from others. This may include allowing someone to pay for my lunch, make me a cup of tea, or complete a household chore such as doing the dishes, which I would normally do myself. At the end of the day, I reflect on how open I was and how it felt to receive.

STEP 12

At the time that is most preferable, I engage in some form of **spiritual practice**. This may include meditation, yoga, journaling, music, Earthing, spiritual development circle, et cetera. During this time I am fully present in the moment.

DAY 6 *Journal*

Did you complete Daily Processes 1-9? How did each step impact your day?

_____

_____

_____

_____

_____

What other steps did you complete today? What felt the most comfortable and/or challenging?

_____

_____

_____

_____

What are your goals for tomorrow?

_____

_____

_____

_____

Day 7

STEPS 1–9
Refer to Daily Processes 1 through 9

STEP 10
I identify and jot down the areas in my life that I wish to **Simplify and Declutter**. This may include physical decluttering, such as clearing out a room or a cupboard, or relationships, or emotional, spiritual, or financial clutter. I then select an item from the list and commence removing the clutter, simplifying my life and making more space for more opportunities to be presented to me. **(Simplify and Declutter, on page 72)**

STEP 11
Today I actively engage in my chosen social media platform by commenting on a post or a feed. The response can be as simple as a "Yes" to a thread or theme that resonates with me. This action helps make me visible in the world of social media, builds confidence, and also enhances the existing community. **(Social Networking, on page 84)**

STEP 12
During the day I write positive affirmations for my wallet, purse, or bag (whatever I use to carry money). I can do this in a variety of ways, including writing affirmations in permanent marker on my wallet, purse, or bag, pinning affirmative notes to my bag, writing on Post-it notes and placing them inside, or even purchasing or making a new wallet, purse, or bag. This action reminds me each time I exchange money that I am already prosperous. **(Positive Affirmation Wallet, on page 49)**

DAY 7 *Journal*

Did you complete Daily Processes 1-9? How did each step impact your day?

_____

_____

_____

_____

_____

What other steps did you complete today? What felt the most comfortable and/or challenging?

_____

_____

_____

_____

What are your goals for tomorrow?

_____

_____

_____

_____

DAY 8

STEPS 1-9
Refer to Daily Processes 1 through 9
STEP 10
Throughout the day, anytime I am dealing with giving or receiving money, I do the **Quick 2-Step Money-Relationship Healing Process**. Refer to Day 1 **(Quick 2-Step Money-Relationship Healing Process, on page 47)**
STEP 11
I find at least one opportunity to be of service today through my time, energy, gifts, abilities, or any other way I may be able to contribute to someone in need.
STEP 12
At the scheduled time, I connect with my friends for our weekly Mastermind Group session. During this safe and supportive time together, we review what we have achieved over the past week and any challenges we may have encountered. We also set our intentions for the following week so we have a plan in moving forward to achieve our desired outcomes. **(Mastermind Group, on page 83)**

Day 8 *Journal*

Did you complete Daily Processes 1-9? How did each step impact your day?

_____

_____

_____

_____

_____

What other steps did you complete today? What felt the most comfortable and/or challenging?

_____

_____

_____

_____

_____

What are your goals for tomorrow?

_____

_____

_____

_____

_____

DAY 9

STEPS 1-9
Refer to Daily Processes 1 through 9

STEP 10
Today I review my **Joy List** and add any other things I have thought of in the last week that bring me joy. I reflect on what has brought me joy in the last week and what actions I have taken to implement practices I had previously noted on my list. (**Joy List, on page 15**)

STEP 11
I make time to reflect on how I am feeling about carrying larger amounts of cash than I would normally do. If I am feeling comfortable, I withdraw additional money, increasing the amount of cash I am carrying. If I am still feeling uncomfortable, I try to identify why (for example, I am afraid I will be robbed, or I am afraid I will lose it). I continue to carry the cash and remind myself that I am fully supported by the Universe. (**Carrying Cash, on page 48**)

STEP 12
I reflect on how I am **Anchoring Balance** between my work and personal life and my actions of the past week to achieve and adopt this as part of my lifestyle. (**Anchoring Balance, on page 66**)

DAY 9 *Journal*

Did you complete Daily Processes 1-9? How did each step impact your day?

_____

_____

_____

_____

_____

What other steps did you complete today? What felt the most comfortable and/or challenging?

_____

_____

_____

_____

_____

What are your goals for tomorrow?

_____

_____

_____

_____

_____

Day 10

STEPS 1–9
Refer to Daily Processes 1 through 9
STEP 10
Today I reflect on how I felt when I committed myself to facing a fear and doing something outside of my comfort zone. I identify how my life may have altered since I took this action (that is, happier, more confident, lighter). If I was not able to follow through with an action, I am gentle on myself and acknowledge that I was at least willing to follow through, which takes me one step closer to completing this action. If I feel comfortable doing so, I take steps today to move forward in achieving this action.
STEP 11
At some time during my day, I set aside time to **Acknowledge My Grandest Vision**. I jot down all the things I aspire to achieve, regardless of how farfetched or unobtainable they may seem. I place no limits, restrictions, or boundaries on my dreams, and I imagine everything I ever dreamed of coming to me. On completion of the list, I take a few moments to set the intent that each item will come into fruition with ease and grace, and I am open to receiving them all.
STEP 12
At the end of the day, I take a few moments to reflect on how I showed **Kindness** to someone today and how kindness was shown to me. I contemplate how I felt at the times I was giving and receiving kindness.

Day 10 *Journal*

Did you complete Daily Processes 1-9? How did each step impact your day?

_____

_____

_____

_____

_____

What other steps did you complete today? What felt the most comfortable and/or challenging?

_____

_____

_____

_____

What are your goals for tomorrow?

_____

_____

_____

_____

Day 11

STEPS 1–9
Refer to Daily Processes 1 through 9
STEP 10
Today I share something on social media that reflects who I am and also inspires others. (**Social Networking, on page 84**)
STEP 11
I honor myself today by selecting something on my list for **Personal Time,** with the intention of relaxing. I may select the same option I chose last week, or do something completely different. I may also add to the list. (**Personal Time, on page 65**)
STEP 12
I reflect today on how I felt giving the **Gift Envelopes,** knowing that I made someone's day with no expectation of anything in return. I place another few Gift Envelopes in different places throughout the day, the more random the better! (**Gift Envelopes, on page 50**)

Day 11 *Journal*

Did you complete Daily Processes 1-9? How did each step impact your day?

_____

_____

_____

_____

_____

What other steps did you complete today? What felt the most comfortable and/or challenging?

_____

_____

_____

_____

What are your goals for tomorrow?

_____

_____

_____

_____

_____

DAY 12

STEPS 1–9

Refer to Daily Processes 1 through 9

STEP 10

I set aside time to go through my **Quality List**. Is there anything I can add or subtract, now that I am conscious of the qualities I already have in my life? I hold the list to my heart area and verbally express my gratitude out loud to the Universe for all the gifts bestowed upon me. **(Quality List, on page 20)**

STEP 11

I notice my breathing patterns again today. Now that I have more awareness about my breathing, am I actively moving toward a deeper breathing pattern? I spend 5 minutes breathing in fully and deeply all the way down to my abdomen and slowly exhale.

STEP 12

I look back over the last week and identify where I have been more fluid in my actions and responses. How did I feel when I relinquished control over an outcome? Was there any type of change? Did I follow through or take control again? Am I compassionate with myself, if I identify that I am challenged by releasing control, and aim to surrender some control today?

DAY 12 *Journal*

Did you complete Daily Processes 1-9? How did each step impact your day?

_____

_____

_____

_____

_____

What other steps did you complete today? What felt the most comfortable and/or challenging?

_____

_____

_____

_____

What are your goals for tomorrow?

_____

_____

_____

_____

_____

Day 13

STEPS 1-9
Refer to Daily Processes 1 through 9

STEP 10
Through the course of the day, I review what steps I have made over the past week to **Build My Business**, adding additional steps I have identified. In reviewing the last week, I also identify what challenges have presented and what I may need to alter to bring me back into alignment with my plan. I develop a loose timeframe for each step, acknowledging that some will take more time and effort than others. **(Building Your Business, on page 68)**

STEP 11
I am open to **Receiving** and consciously accept an offer from someone to do something for me today. At the end of my day, I assess how well I have used my **Receiving** muscles and identify any opportunities where I may have used them better (for example, I was offered a beverage but chose to get my own, in addition to making one for someone else!).

STEP 12
Today I set aside 15 to 30 minutes to meditate. I sit or lie down in a place where I will not be disturbed, either indoors or in Nature, and just be. I do not judge or chastise myself if my mind races or wanders, as I know that I am still receiving healthy benefits from meditation just by ceasing all other activities. If I am able, I may extend the amount of time I dedicate to this process.

DAY 13 *Journal*

Did you complete Daily Processes 1-9? How did each step impact your day?

What other steps did you complete today? What felt the most comfortable and/or challenging?

What are your goals for tomorrow?

DAY 14

STEPS 1–9

Refer to Daily Processes 1 through 9

STEP 10

I make time today to remove clutter. This might be as extensive as spring cleaning or a simpler task, such as cleaning out my wallet/purse and removing any items that are no longer required (for example, old receipts, expired credit cards, business cards that are no longer important, any objects that need a more appropriate home—data cards/sticks, and old keys that are no longer used). **(Simplify and Declutter, on page 72)**

STEP 11

CONGRATULATIONS!!! You are halfway through the Prosperity Plan. Today I celebrate this wonderful achievement by doing a **Gratitude Dance**. I gather together my list of gratitudes from the Gratitude Game (Day 3), find a device I can play music on, and choose a happy, upbeat song that I love. I hold my gratitudes over my heart area, and take a moment to set the intention of giving gratitude to the Universe for all that I have. I turn on my song, and dance! While dancing, I say or sing all the items on my list! When the song finishes, I take another moment to thank the Universe for everything that I have. If I am feeling in the mood, I repeat this process again with as many songs as I wish. **(Gratitude Game, on page 94)**

STEP 12

To expand upon the theme of celebrating, today I host a social mixer so I can share my success with others. This may be as simple as going to the movies with a few friends, having a picnic, or throwing a dinner party. **(Host a Social Mixer, on page 85)**

Day 14 *Journal*

Did you complete Daily Processes 1-9? How did each step impact your day?

_____

_____

_____

_____

_____

What other steps did you complete today? What felt the most comfortable and/or challenging?

_____

_____

_____

_____

What are your goals for tomorrow?

_____

_____

_____

_____

Day 15

STEPS 1–9
Refer to Daily Processes 1 through 9

STEP 10
Throughout the day, any time I am dealing with giving or receiving money I do the **Quick 2-Step Money-Relationship Healing Process**. Refer to Day 1 **(Quick 2-Step Money-Relationship Healing Process, on page 47)**

STEP 11
I find at least one opportunity to be of service today through my time, energy, gifts, abilities, or any other way I may be able to contribute to someone in need.

STEP 12
At the scheduled time, I connect with a few friends for our weekly Mastermind Group session. During this safe and supportive time together, we review what we have achieved over the past week and any challenges we may have encountered. We also set our intentions for the following week so we have a plan in moving forward to achieve our desired outcomes. **(Mastermind Group, on page 83)**

Day 15 *Journal*

Did you complete Daily Processes 1-9? How did each step impact your day?

_____

_____

_____

_____

_____

What other steps did you complete today? What felt the most comfortable and/or challenging?

_____

_____

_____

_____

What are your goals for tomorrow?

_____

_____

_____

_____

DAY 16

STEPS 1–9
Refer to Daily Processes 1 through 9

STEP 10
Today I review my **Joy List** and add any other things I have thought of in the last week that bring me joy. I reflect on what has brought me joy in the last week and what actions I have taken to implement practices I had previously put on my list. (**Joy List, on page** 15)

STEP 11
Can I add more to the amount of cash I am carrying today? Am I becoming more comfortable carrying extra cash around with me? If so, then I carry a larger amount, if I am able. (**Carrying Cash, on page** 48)

STEP 12
How have I handled my work/life balance today? Did one aspect hold greater sway than another (for example, choosing to stay behind at work rather than spending time with family and friends, or canceling a scheduled class or practice that brings me joy to complete a work task)? (**Anchoring Balance, on page 66**)

Day 16 *Journal*

Did you complete Daily Processes 1-9? How did each step impact your day?

_____

_____

_____

_____

What other steps did you complete today? What felt the most comfortable and/or challenging?

_____

_____

_____

_____

What are your goals for tomorrow?

_____

_____

_____

_____

DAY 17

STEPS 1-9

Refer to Daily Processes 1 through 9

STEP 10

I am willing to develop my intuition today by allowing my spirit to lead me rather than my mind. When I come across a decision to be made during the course of the day, I gratefully acknowledge my mind's response, but then I ask myself how I *feel* about the answer. I am open to receiving information that flows from my spirit. I follow this guidance and witness how this plays out for me.

STEP 11

Today I reflect on how I am feeling about voluntarily repaying all or part of a debt, prior to being asked or before the due date, regardless of the amount I repay. I make an additional payment today that's slightly larger than my last voluntary payment, even if it is only a small amount greater.

STEP 12

Throughout the course of the day, I smile at all the people who cross my path, whether they are known to me or not. I look them in the eyes, establishing a connection with them, and genuinely smile at them from my heart. **(Smiling, on page 96)**

DAY 17 *Journal*

Did you complete Daily Processes 1-9? How did each step impact your day?

_____

_____

_____

_____

_____

What other steps did you complete today? What felt the most comfortable and/or challenging?

_____

_____

_____

_____

What are your goals for tomorrow?

_____

_____

_____

_____

DAY 18

STEPS 1–9

Refer to Daily Processes 1 through 9

STEP 10

I post and comment on my chosen social network platform today. I also sign up to attend a free event I am interested in, broadening my social media network. **(Social Networking, on page 84)**

STEP 11

At some point during my day, I conduct research on any courses or workshops I am interested in, whether in-person or online. If appropriate, I formally schedule a time to observe a class to gain a better understanding of what is involved and to see if it resonates with me in the same way it does on paper or the Internet.

STEP 12

I reflect again today on how I felt giving the **Gift Envelopes**, knowing that I made someone's day with no expectation of anything in return. I place another few Gift Envelopes in different places throughout the day, the more random the better! **(Gift Envelopes, on page 50)**

DAY 18 *Journal*

Did you complete Daily Processes 1-9? How did each step impact your day?

_____

_____

_____

_____

_____

What other steps did you complete today? What felt the most comfortable and/or challenging?

_____

_____

_____

_____

What are your goals for tomorrow?

_____

_____

_____

_____

DAY 19

STEPS 1–9
Refer to Daily Processes 1 through 9

STEP 10
I set aside time to go through my **Quality List**. Is there anything I can add or subtract, now that I am conscious of the qualities I already have in my life? I hold the list to my heart area and verbally express my gratitude out loud to the Universe for all the gifts bestowed upon me. **(Quality List, on page 20)**

STEP 11
I focus on my **Breathing**, taking full and deep breaths as I move through my day. If I notice that I am taking small shallow breaths, I stop what I am doing and take a few moments to concentrate on breathing deeply. (Refer to Day 5)

STEP 12
I find at least one opportunity to be of service today through my time, energy, gifts, abilities, or any other way I may be able to contribute to someone in need.

Day 19 *Journal*

Did you complete Daily Processes 1-9? How did each step impact your day?

_____

_____

_____

_____

_____

What other steps did you complete today? What felt the most comfortable and/or challenging?

_____

_____

_____

_____

What are your goals for tomorrow?

_____

_____

_____

_____

DAY 20

STEPS 1–9

Refer to Daily Processes 1 through 9

STEP 10

At the start of my day, I stand in front of the mirror and say out loud, "**I am open to receiving today.**" As I verbalize my intent out loud, I am further affirming, anchoring, and setting into motion my intention for the day to come.

STEP 11

If I run my own business or would like to do so, I review my list of actions to build my business and evaluate my progress so far. I may also choose to register my business name, create a business page on a social media platform, create a business plan, join a business networking group or forum, or even open a bank account that will be solely dedicated to my business. (**Building Your Business, on page 68**)

STEP 12

I make time during the day to read an article based on a spiritual practice or a few chapters of a spiritually based book.
Alternatively, I may listen to a recording or a podcast of a spiritual leader on a topic that is of interest to me.

DAY 20 *Journal*

Did you complete Daily Processes 1-9? How did each step impact your day?

_____

_____

_____

_____

What other steps did you complete today? What felt the most comfortable and/or challenging?

_____

_____

_____

_____

What are your goals for tomorrow?

_____

_____

_____

_____

Day 21

STEPS 1–9
Refer to Daily Processes 1 through 9

STEP 10
I make the time today to reflect on the relationships I have in my life and whether they are serving my highest good. For example: Do I have any friends or family whom I seem always to be "giving" to, without receiving anything in return? Are there people in my life who always make negative comments and leave me feeling exhausted or deflated? Are there people in my life who consistently disrespect me by crossing inappropriate boundaries, despite repeated requests not to? Once I have identified these people, I express my gratitude for the lessons and blessings they have previously brought into my life and gently release them, opening myself for healthier relationships to be created in my life. **(Simplify and Declutter, on page 72)**

STEP 11
Today I reach out to other social network users and ask them to "like" or "follow" me on my chosen social network platform. **(Social Networking, on page 84)**

STEP 12
Throughout the course of my day, I smile at all the people who cross my path, whether I know them or not. I look them in the eyes, establishing a connection with them, and genuinely smile at them from my heart. I notice and acknowledge their response and how it makes me feel to smile with genuine intent at others. **(Smiling, on page 96)**

DAY 21 *Journal*

Did you complete Daily Processes 1-9? How did each step impact your day?

_____

_____

_____

_____

_____

What other steps did you complete today? What felt the most comfortable and/or challenging?

_____

_____

_____

_____

_____

What are your goals for tomorrow?

_____

_____

_____

_____

_____

DAY 22

STEPS 1-9
Refer to Daily Processes 1 through 9

STEP 10
Throughout the day, anytime I am dealing with giving or receiving money, I do the **Quick 2-Step Money-Relationship Healing Process.** Refer to Day 1 **(Quick 2-Step Money-Relationship Healing Process, on page 47)**

STEP 11
I find at least one opportunity to be of service today through my time, energy, gifts, abilities, or any other way I may be able to contribute to someone in need.

STEP 12
At the scheduled time, I connect with a few friends for our weekly Mastermind Group session. During this safe and supportive time together, we review what we have achieved over the past week and any challenges we may have encountered. We also set our intentions for the following week so we have a plan in moving forward to achieve our desired outcomes. **(Mastermind Group, on page 83)**

DAY 22 *Journal*

Did you complete Daily Processes 1-9? How did each step impact your day?

_____

_____

_____

_____

_____

What other steps did you complete today? What felt the most comfortable and/or challenging?

_____

_____

_____

_____

What are your goals for tomorrow?

_____

_____

_____

_____

DAY 23

| STEPS 1-9 |
| Refer to Daily Processes 1 through 9 |

| STEP 10 |
| I add to my **Joy List** today and celebrate my willingness to be open to receiving joy in my life by doing something special that represents joy to me. This can be something simple, such as watching my favorite movie at the end of my day or buying myself a bunch of flowers, or something more extravagant, such as dressing up and going out for a meal or booking a holiday. (**Joy List, on page 15**) |

| STEP 11 |
| I ask myself today how I am feeling about carrying extra cash by referring back to Week 1, when I first commenced increasing the amount of cash I carry with me every day. I increase the amount again, if I can comfortably do that. (**Carrying Cash, on page 48**) |

| STEP 12 |
| At some time today, I review my **Grandest Vision** list and identify whether I can add or remove items. I hold it to my heart and express my gratitude to the Universe for bringing these items to me, now and in the future, trusting that all will come to fruition. |

DAY 23 *Journal*

Did you complete Daily Processes 1-9? How did each step impact your day?

_____

_____

_____

_____

_____

What other steps did you complete today? What felt the most comfortable and/or challenging?

_____

_____

_____

_____

_____

What are your goals for tomorrow?

_____

_____

_____

_____

DAY 24

STEPS 1-9

Refer to Daily Processes 1 through 9

STEP 10

Today I ask myself the question, "Am I more comfortable facing my fears, knowing that it is the mind's way of keeping me safe, and taking actions outside of my comfort zone?" To answer this question, I consider my fears and the actions I have taken to overcome them while enacting this plan, acknowledging my achievements and how I felt after I had overcome my fears. I also identify and acknowledge that some of my fears may still trigger me, though my intent moving forward is to connect with my feelings and not my mind, which may prove easier in facing my fears. I stand in front of the mirror, look myself in the eye, and say out loud "**I am fearless.**"

STEP 11

At some point in my day, I reflect on how my life has been altered by my being willing to actively repay a debt. Did I suffer or go without in any way? Did repaying the debt put my life on hold in any way? Did I feel good when I made the payment? After I have answered these questions, I congratulate myself on the progress I have made, showing the Universe that I am grateful and moving forward to becoming debt-free.

STEP 12

It's time to play the **Gratitude Game** again today! To expand on my feelings of gratitude for all I have, I identify all that I am grateful for, both small and large, and share them with my family, friends, colleagues, and via social media. I openly invite others to share their gratitudes with me. **(Gratitude Game, on page 94)**

DAY 24 *Journal*

Did you complete Daily Processes 1-9? How did each step impact your day?

_____

_____

_____

_____

_____

What other steps did you complete today? What felt the most comfortable and/or challenging?

_____

_____

_____

_____

What are your goals for tomorrow?

_____

_____

_____

_____

DAY 25

STEPS 1–9
Refer to Daily Processes 1 through 9

STEP 10
Today I comment on a minimum of five (5) posts from items that appear in my newsfeed on social media that evoke a positive feeling or that resonate with me. **(Social Networking, on page 84)**

STEP 11
On this day, I make a commitment to myself. I commit that when I am the recipient of unexpected or additional income, instead of spending it all on luxury items, I allocate it to an investment in myself. This may include further education or equipment required to achieve my grandest vision or, if appropriate, to build my business.

STEP 12
During the day, I discreetly leave a **Gift Envelope** for someone I am aware lacks confidence, is often overlooked, has low self-esteem, or is going through challenging times. This may be a work colleague, family member or friend, or someone such as the person who checks out my groceries or my bus driver. **(Gift Envelopes, on page 50)**

DAY 25 *Journal*

Did you complete Daily Processes 1-9? How did each step impact your day?

_____

_____

_____

_____

_____

What other steps did you complete today? What felt the most comfortable and/or challenging?

_____

_____

_____

_____

What are your goals for tomorrow?

_____

_____

_____

_____

DAY 26

STEPS 1–9

Refer to Daily Processes 1 through 9

STEP 10

Today I set aside some time to review and reflect on the **Quality List** I created at the start of the Prosperity Plan. I ask myself if it is now easier to identify the qualities each of my lifestyle activities brings into my life and which areas in my life are not attracting any of the qualities I desire. I then allow myself to make the decision, guided by my intuition, to release activities, behaviors, and patterns that are constrictive and not expansive. **(Quality List, on page 20)**

STEP 11

Today I reflect on how my breathing patterns have changed since commencing the Prosperity Plan and the difference it makes to my overall well-being.

STEP 12

During the day I contemplate on **Anchoring Balance** in my life and how my lifestyle has changed over the last month, due to the positive steps I am taking to achieve a healthier work/life balance. I show myself compassion if I have been met with challenges, as the timing may be slightly inappropriate to fully explore this process due to previous commitments, such as a heightened work peak that I have committed to and already made allowances for, prior to commencing the **28-Day Prosperity Plan**. **(Anchoring Balance, on page 66)**

Day 26 *Journal*

Did you complete Daily Processes 1-9? How did each step impact your day?

_____

_____

_____

_____

_____

What other steps did you complete today? What felt the most comfortable and/or challenging?

_____

_____

_____

_____

_____

What are your goals for tomorrow?

_____

_____

_____

_____

_____

DAY 27

| STEPS 1–9 |
| Refer to Daily Processes 1 through 9 |

| STEP 10 |
| Today I celebrate the baby steps, or if my business is established, the expansion of my business that has resulted in my commitment to make time to focus on my business each week. **(Building Your Business, on page 68)** |

| STEP 11 |
| At the end of my day, I reflect on how many compliments I received today and how I felt when I received them. I express my gratitude for being open to receive them and for feeling more and more comfortable each time. |

| STEP 12 |
| Today I engage in a spiritual practice with others. I might attend a yoga or meditation class, tai chi group, or a spiritual development circle. In this way I am opening myself up to different experiences to identify what practice resonates with me the most and that I would like to pursue further. I may also attend a class with a different teacher if I have already implemented these practices into my life. |

DAY 27 *Journal*

Did you complete Daily Processes 1-9? How did each step impact your day?

_____

_____

_____

_____

_____

What other steps did you complete today? What felt the most comfortable and/or challenging?

_____

_____

_____

_____

What are your goals for tomorrow?

_____

_____

_____

_____

_____

DAY 28

STEPS 1-9

Refer to Daily Processes 1 through 9

STEP 10

I reflect on the changes that have occurred since I commenced the process to **Simplify and Declutter** my life. I identify new opportunities that have presented, new friendships or relationships (including with myself), and my overall sense of well-being. **(Simplify and Declutter, on page 72)**

STEP 11

I take a few minutes today to answer the questions, "What does prosperity mean to me?" and "What does money mean to me?" and jot down the first thoughts that come into my mind.
I compare these answers to those I wrote on Day 1 of the Prosperity Plan and reflect on how I have changed and grown over the past 28 days.

STEP 12

Today I celebrate completing the **28-Day Prosperity Plan** by doing a Gratitude Dance! **(Gratitude Dance, on page 95)**

DAY 28 *Journal*

Did you complete Daily Processes 1-9? How did each step impact your day?

_____

_____

_____

_____

_____

What other steps did you complete today? What felt the most comfortable and/or challenging?

_____

_____

_____

_____

What are your goals for tomorrow?

_____

_____

_____

_____

_____

AFTERWORD

MONEY IS A part of prosperity, but it isn't the only part.

By reading this book, you have been initiated into the idea that we can promote prosperity by treating it kindly and lovingly, as the Divine being that it is. We can now see money as energy that is sacred and spiritual. This helps us to remember that we are worthy of having money, just as we are worthy of receiving all sacred gifts.

Feel free to personalize the processes in this book. Choose the prosperity methods that feel best to you, to help keep you in alignment with the Universe. Mark up, underline, and highlight the ideas in this book. Make this book your own. It might help you to make up some of your own processes, once you get a feel for how to connect to the Universe's prosperity energy.

Even though this book has come to an end, it doesn't mean that our journey is over. As you've read the ideas and processes in this book, your intention to create greater prosperity in your life has been set. Don't allow yourself to just set this book down and forget about these processes. This is your compact field guide to a more prosperous and happier life. Take it with you wherever you go and refer to it. Carry its teachings with you. The more you integrate these processes into your daily life, the more they can work for you in empowering ways.

One of the main reasons I wrote *Easy Breezy Prosperity* was because there is *still* a strong notion, especially in many spiritual circles, that money somehow is not spiritual. I can completely empathize with this view, because it's one that I used to carry with me also.

When you think of, hear about, or see images that depict financial abundance, do you cringe or get offended in any way? If you don't, then I am so grateful to know that you have done the inner work to expand yourself into greater states of understanding when it comes to your experience with money. However, if you do get offended when something relating to money enters your experience, maybe it's time to take a closer look at why this is happening.

To heal any antipathy we may have toward money, it is important to understand what money actually is and to know its purpose. Everything in the Universe has a unique energy signature, meaning that everything in the Universe is a living, breathing entity. Some energy signatures may appear to be more alive than others, because they manifest themselves in louder ways. We clearly see this in human beings and the animal kingdom. However, even though the plant or mineral kingdoms may not have as "loud" a personality, they are still fully alive and thriving. So if everything is alive, then money itself is not a lifeless object. It is actually a living, breathing energy here to coexist with other living, breathing beings.

Imagine if you projected the beliefs you have about money on to your best friend by saying, "You are not spiritual, you cause problems, you are bad and evil, you are not enough, and you are just a lifeless object. I feel guilty for being around you. People have to struggle, fight, cheat, steal, and work very hard to have you in their lives." Wow! Think about how traumatized your best friend would be if you projected all of this on to them for years and years! I know that if this were happening to me, my desire would be to run in the opposite direction of the person who was abusing me in that way.

Well, my friend, this is exactly what we have been doing to money, especially when we see it as being anything less than spiritual.

This realization completely changed my life. I started to see that by projecting my own judgments on to this living, breathing energy, I was in fact moving myself away from the spiritual path I so desired to experience. After going through a grieving phase as a result of realizing how badly I was treating money, I started forgiving myself and asking the energy of money to forgive me for not knowing any better at the time.

I then began asking money itself questions like, "How can I support you, love you, nurture you, serve you, heal you, and bless you even more?" I had never thought to ask these types of questions before. Up to that point, it was always about me, me, me and focusing on my own insecurities when it came to my relationship with money.

Imagine asking your best friend questions like the ones I just mentioned. They would probably want to be around you all the time. Thankfully, this is exactly what began to occur in my life with how I experienced money. I started attracting more of it, because I was treating it like I would a kindred friend.

As I have mentioned, money itself is a living, breathing energy that is here to fulfill its purpose of being the embodiment of giving and receiving, just as we are here to fulfill our own purpose. Like the principles of gravity, aerodynamics, attraction, and much more, there is also a principle of circulation. Money is the physical representation of the exchange that takes place during the principle of circulation, which is all about the natural flow of giving and receiving energy. That's all it is!

So with this new understanding, we can actually see that money has been spiritual all along. All of those misconceptions we placed around money had absolutely nothing to do with money and everything to do with our own behavior toward it.

The next time a thought appears in your consciousness that money is anything less than spiritual, use it as an opportunity to experience a huge breakthrough. The mind likes to stay in its comfort zone, and many of the misconceptions we have around money are just the mind's way of protecting itself, making it feel safe and secure so it does not have to look outside itself. The triggers we feel when the word "money" comes up are indicators that something within us is looking to expand.

It's our birthright to be abundant and prosperous. It is part of the well-being we get to experience in this world. The Universe itself is a vast, unlimited, and ever-expanding energy, so why would we think we are anything less than that?

I hope these words have given you a new perspective to consider that will ultimately support you in finally being at peace with your experience of money and financial abundance. Money needs our compassion, support, and love. This is how we will heal it from the trauma it has endured for thousands of years and what will heal our relationship with money once and for all.

Easy Breezy Prosperity is here to help you, no matter what your emotional state or outer circumstances. If you're feeling down, it can help bring balance to your life and promote prosperity within you. Remember that once you start implementing the changes, it can take 21 days to break a habit and 28 days to make a new one—so persevere.

Please feel free to share this book with your friends and family, as I have shared it with you. As you know, circulation is a powerful principle that works in beautiful ways that we will never fully comprehend. Allow it to pursue its goals.

I am honored to have shared this amazing journey with you. I believe in you and wish great joy for you and the fulfillment of your dreams, your life path, and your vision of a beautiful and prosperous life.

May prosperity rain upon you always!

Love,

Emmanuel

Further Reading

Breathnach, Sarah Ban. *Simple Abundance: A Daybook of Comfort and Joy.* New York: Grand Central Publishing, 2009.

Coelho, Paulo. *The Alchemist.* San Francisco: HarperOne, 2014.

Dyer, Wayne. *Wishes Fulfilled: Mastering the Art of Manifesting.* Carlsbad, CA: Hay House, 2013.

Eker, T. Harv. *Secrets of the Millionaire Mind: Mastering the Inner Game of Wealth.* New York: HarperBusiness, 2005.

Hay, Louise. *You Can Heal Your Life.* 2nd ed. Carlsbad, CA: Hay House, 1984.

Hicks, Jerry and Esther. *Ask and It Is Given: Learning to Manifest Your Dreams.* Carlsbad, CA: Hay House, 2004.

Hill, Napoleon. *Think and Grow Rich.* rev. ed. Los Angeles: Tarcher, 2005.

Ling, Kristi. *Operation Happiness.* Rodale, 2016.

Ruiz, Don Miguel. *The Four Agreements.* San Rafael, CA: Amber Allen, 1997.

Tolle, Eckhart. *The Power of Now.* Vancouver, BC: Namaste Publishing, 2004.

Walsch, Neale Donald. *The Little Soul and the Sun.* Newburyport, MA: Hampton Roads Publishing, 1998.

These pages can be used in whatever way you feel is best on your Prosperity Journey. You may use them for daily journal entries or as a place to store thoughts, feelings, and epiphanies as they come up. It is totally up to you!